# 77 Written reasons to stop looking at models who do video chat online

C Borşe

Published by C Borşe, 2024.

# Also by C Borșe

77 Written reasons to stop looking at models who do video chat online

C. Borse

# 77 written reasons to stop watching and talking to online video chat models

Sight dominates most senses

## How to be conscious of your wasted time when you're online on an adult video chat website

The author of this book does not issue medical advice or prescribe the use of any technique as a form of treatment for physical, emotional or medical problems without the advice of a physician, either directly or indirectly. The author's intention is only to provide training of a general nature to assist you in your quest for physical, spiritual, and emotional well-being. If you use any of the information in this book for your purposes, the author and publisher assume no responsibility for your actions. The book is not suitable for people under 18.

Release date: February 2024

CIP Description of the National Library of Romania
BORSE, C.
  77 written reasons to stop watching and talking to online video chat models / C. Borse – Bucharest; 2024
  ISBN:

C. Borse

# 77 written reasons to stop watching and talking to online video chat models

The real reasons why one enters adult video chat, as well as the reasons why one works on video chat as a model

# How do you be conscious of your wasted time when you're online on a an adult website with video chat

Bucharest 2024

# Summary

The content of this book is a manifesto against the beliefs and convictions of some people who use the internet, go on adult websites, video chat, look at models showing nudity, strip and many other behaviours that pertain to adult websites. The book is for people who *can't* or *don't know how* to give up video chatting, even if the reason tells them that this activity is unhealthy and stressful. Some people are thinking about giving up watching models doing video chat but can't give it up. Many people who hang out on video chat sites will continue to log on quite often, either during the day, evening, or night. Some people say they will never go on a video chat site again or stop, but they will continue doing it. Many people cannot control themselves, and they can't prevent unhealthy conduct. People are motivated to act by their senses, for how they feel and how they feel after they choose to do that thing, which can often be undermined as pleasurable gratification. That's not to say that there aren't people who can't control themselves about watching models or models doing/doing video chat.

The force of the impulse arising in the body, which some people call energy, and the thoughts of the people in their fantasies and intentions to be on video chat are often clandestine because senses arise spontaneously in the body and mind of the person who desires to enter a video chat website. Thoughts come from our thought processes, beliefs, and emotions to believe in something being talked about or done. A behaviour that has many episodes in which one cannot control the use of a substance, or has a harmful behaviour that is frequent, repeating itself several times in a year, and turns into a form of addiction. This behaviour called addiction is repeated for something or after something, after which its addictive state controls the body and mind.

Where does this form of addiction come from?

From inside our bodies, through our emotions and feelings, which often control our behaviour and beliefs, to believe in something, do something, or consume something frequently. What I have written about and how I have written it can be complex, and I have chosen a description by stating the reasons. I have tried to present the behaviour of people who frequently enter video chat to feel psychological satisfaction due to desire or a form of addiction, which controls the will of some people. Don't let unhealthy emotions and feelings influence your behaviour against your will. I am addressing people who know it is harmful to stay on video chat but cannot let go. The reasons described in the book may or may not help in quitting video chat. Further, only you can make that choice. More details about people in this video chat industry are written on the following pages.

Why did I write this way in this little book? Some people are influenced to do certain things in a type of behaviour and often regret addictive behaviours and are unaware that they are addicted. I say it's an addiction because that behaviour, throughout life, is repeated for years and years because of the lifestyle they choose to live.

Living with suffering isn't healthy!

*Everyone is important to whom you say you are, and no excellent paying people work in video chat studios or do this work from home.*

*Paying money for people to expose themselves somewhere on a monitor doesn't help.*

*The impulse you feel to join a video chat site comes from within you, and if you understand your feelings, when you feel that impulse, you have the power to stop.*

*Misunderstood emotions, by chance, can lead to changes for better or worse in a person's life.*

*What is written here and how it is written is aimed at most people. I am aware that opinions differ, so take what you think. You may find it helpful.*

Note: Please be aware of how I chose to describe the words video chat split or video chat linked, which is optional.

# Part I

# Introduction

It is possibly a start for people who instinctively think and feel it's not good to look at an adult or non-adult online video chat website and spend money. But it's not just the spending of money that I bring to this discussion; it's the benefit of doing something else healthy and beneficial with that time spent on a video chat site by replacing a harmful habit with a healthy one. For the reasons described, I try to help, in my way, people who feel intuitively and want to understand the change of thinking and behaviour, replacing it with rational thought so that they stop frequenting models who do video chat. Only he, she or they can choose what they could replace that useless time spent on erotic video chat with; I say erotic because one ends up wanting eroticism by relating to video chat models. In the way I wrote, I meant no disrespect to those who do video chat or those who pay for video chat. I believe we are all responsible for the decisions and choices we make in life.

I have chosen to expose, with arguments and descriptions, my opinions about video chat, this unhealthy and harmful activity on the psyche and behaviour.

People who think they're relaxing with video chat models, the person who often goes on video chat, keep this side isolated and hidden, so they are not visible in reality and do not have conversations... about video chat.

There are no discussions between people who pay video chat models; I don't know of any forum or web pages where the consequences of frequenting video chat models are discussed. Significantly, few people in the video chat industry pay for video chat models; I have heard them talk openly about what they do after entering video chat to watch those working in video chat studios or from home. I'm not writing out of hate or revenge; I'm writing because these are people who spend their time and have spent money and will continue to spend money on video chat models. I write for those people so that they can control their impulses as best they can regarding online video chat and stay as far away from online video chat models as possible. I am talking about the modest people, not the rich people who, after a while, gave up because of the money spent and realised that time and money were wasted, which is an unpleasant feeling, but life goes on.

If you read the written reasons and find them unclear, some may be appropriate for someone else. People have different opinions and beliefs, so I have tried to fit in as best I knew so that the reasons are generally described for more than one category of person. I am not saying that I make no mistakes as I write. They are understood as mistakes in expression and perceived differently, or I am wrong, and I apologise if anything is unclear in what follows.

This book, which does not have a large number of pages, wants to show you and help you understand where you are, the diversity of your thinking, looking at your values, you deserve to respect yourself and take care of yourself healthily. Respecting yourself doesn't mean that there is always a need to feel sensational or that well-being is even more comfortable than you think and that well-being is something special. I mean that feeling that leads to excitement becomes a routine after a while, and you and your mind and body influence that. That desired moment leads you to feel something that feels nice and warm, but that leads you towards losing control of your senses and desires, which is what you want from the beginning regarding the satisfaction of male ejaculation. This desire for satisfaction leads many men to enter video chat. When you feel you need to get on video chat, you'd better be clear that you need to stop, or if you can't, then you'll understand later that it's no longer worth it to go private with models who do video chat.

Some older people have regrets that they didn't do that thing or go in a different direction in life. They have regrets and have wondered where they went wrong and why they didn't speak up at times or that they repeatedly did something that, after a while, is harmful. For the human body to do something driven by fantasy and, daily or almost daily, throughout life is unfavourable, and I am referring to some unhealthy habits and a form of addiction, such as sitting and watching models doing video chat. The reasons described are to reduce or stop time on video chat, which is not healthy and is not something that leads to the future, to a career, to something that will produce or bear fruit, but is a waste of time for people looking to sit on video chat and pay to see naked women. It is better to avoid frequent video chats and ignore people who work in video chat; it is not necessary or healthy to watch the

video chat.

# Why I wrote this book

## The following are a few examples, and then some, about video chat.

I know some people stay on video chat. Generally, guys and men are looking to get on video chat online, but some men want to stop the acquired habit of watching models doing video chat. I am writing for those men who live alone or wish they had a girlfriend or wife, like those models they choose to look at on video chat. While talking to models who do video chat, many clients must realise they deviate from? By turning their imagination into an illusion, clients seek satisfaction only for a few moments.

Long periods of video chat lead to addiction, just as men are addicted to cigarettes and tell many young people not to smoke because it's not healthy, just as there are people who are addicted to alcohol and tell others to stop drinking, just as many people masturbate and can't stop masturbating and are ashamed to tell other people about it just as there are people who use drugs and are addicted and can't stop using that substance, and tell others to stop using drugs.

Some men search the internet, looking for and finding, as they wish, those who work as models in video chat studios or from home —— some people who frequent video chat hope they will have such a person to live with one day.

Many men sit on video chat and wish their partner or wife was like the one on the monitor. Some men look at women who are there and, looking at them, decide what kind of woman they want, but that doesn't mean everyone wants that. Younger teens are curious to see a woman move for them in the monitor, and they want to observe their bodies and what women look like when they're in the place set up for video chat. On the internet and video chat sites, men will find women pleasing and attractive and will be convinced they are worth watching next. The man's mind keeps him on the site and takes him further, to masturbation, to completion, after which, on the next attempt on video chat, he has new thoughts and ideas, often asking for more from the model or models they are talking to.

Some men have new demands; they want to see more in a woman through the monitor, they want to be shown more, then they have to pay a price which they produce, and they don't mind, but they don't realise that the desire to see the same kind of woman working in video chat will be repeated. After a while, it may become a routine, a habit, and then they sense that something is wrong and realise that their intuition and body are telling them that it's something unhealthy. There may be some regret after that pleasure, after being online, because, in reality, he doesn't see that. He only has a few hours of watching models doing video chat online. The person who is in the habit of going to a video chat website often has times when they stop going in to watch video chat models, but they don't tell anyone. Perhaps it works the first time, but after a while, he returns and can't stop himself from going online on video chat, so he goes in again. Even if he doesn't spend any money and ends up wanting that feeling in his body again, which leads to completion. This is the hard-to-deny requirement of the man's mind to reach a pleasurable sensation, to reach orgasm, that is, that climax of the man's sensation when he ejaculates, to have satisfaction. But not everyone needs that kind of satisfaction. Some people are content to watch and talk to models who do video chat and pay them just because they are set up to be beautiful.

Very interestingly, compared to animals who generally respect the mating season of the year, we humans do not; we cannot appreciate the intention to stop ejaculating. In my belief, I believe that ejaculating daily or every week, a few times, leads to addiction and destruction of the body, slowly killing both mentally and physically.

I prefer to write how I see reality in my way, a truth that often doesn't look good or, as I wrote, doesn't look good for people who frequent video chat. That's not to say that all people who get on video chat and spend their money privately have the same reasons to get online and interact in chat. In general, people who have a habit of joining online video chat also join other adult sites, and only they know what they are doing. It is likely inappropriate for many people, going against the beliefs of people who habitually sit and watch models doing video chat. People who don't want to know what I've written about and why I've written it, to learn more about this faulty behaviour controlled by the senses of every individual who wants satisfaction, would ignore me.

Why did I write this book? To show a way and to show that private conversations with video chatters are unhealthy. If a person doesn't understand that at the core is the feeling, which is often incomprehensible to many people, what the body feels, or how it feels, like an emotion or feeling, they need to know that these are significant factors in people's behaviour.

The state of the body is influenced by how it perceives things from the outside in the places where it is, relative to what is happening or what it is discussing. Emotion gives an impulse in the body, inducing what it does, i.e. an emotion persuades it, through their thinking, to believe that it is right to do that thing, for example, to go in and sit on the video chat, because it feels something when it is on the video chat, it wants something specific. If he doesn't understand, he needs to know that to change his emotions, he needs to change his beliefs, and finally, he needs to believe the idea that it's not good to be on video chat; otherwise,e he can't understand what I've written. You can also write the other way around about emotions, i.e. maybe he believes that he needs to satisfy himself when he's on video chat in private.

Emotions are short-lived affective reactions, accompanied by the body's activities, mirroring the attitude towards reality; they start from inside the body. Emotion is felt when you experience an affective state, which is unconscious or conscious, like that for video chat. You want to feel good, or you want to see something nice because some men's lives, in reality, are devoid of women or the woman they want. Emotions control people in some moments of the day, moments when they would like to feel good, I mean video chat, and they are described in words for the reasons described.

I have written about a conscious or unconscious emotion and will give an example. Before entering a video chat, the person who enters is eager to see people who do video chat and ends up, after a few minutes or an hour, masturbating

and after it is over,

becomes frustrated for what he did but still does not understand his desire; why did he enter to see those models who do video chat? I say that because, at first, he may not have gone in with the urge to masturbate but fell for pleasure in its form of love expressed through masturbation or however you want to describe it. If he does this, it is a form of addiction, like someone who consumes alcohol daily but does not intend to be drunk and drinks alcohol because his body demands it. I will describe it as hedonistic behaviour.

Or can it be the case that people believe that faith acts as they think, and if so, then what about anger or hurt feelings? Where do these emotions come from? Where does a diagnosis of, say, anxiety depression come from after a clinical assessment? I wrote the word feeling, and I don't want to describe it in detail because I think it would look more complicated in the mind and thinking of the person reading here; it's not about doing psychological therapy.

If one were to ask: Why does an emotion or feeling influence our thinking or belief in something, that things in life look a certain way as some people understand? That is, people's thinking is influenced by how their mind reflects what is happening around them, being in a connection between the unconscious processes they go through and what they feel at those moments.

For example, why do the impulse and desire instantly arise in a person's mind and body to enter and talk to people or models doing erotic video chat or on an adult website? If you like, write down five answers on a sheet of paper; if you have got to reading, write them down on the next page. Or, if you don't want to write it down, don't.

# What I think about video chat

Video chat is a business and entertainment web service where two or more people interact from different parts of the world. It is a virtual space that allows internet users to communicate with each other via audio as well as video, but I don't mean this type of interaction. The definition of video chat differs from culture to culture, but in the end, they are similar; below, I will write more clearly what I mean.

I'm talking about adult, erotic live, online video chat between people who work as models for clients and people who want to pay for that service by watching video chat, and I say that because I don't think there is anyone who will do video chat as a model for free. People who work have a specific purpose or personal reasons why they're out there live on different video chat sites. It's not only women who do erotic or adult video chat; there are also single people and people with different sexual orientations or couples, and it seems that people who work in video chat are like actresses or actors when they are on video chat because they know what the customers want and they behave in such a way that they attract them. These people have several reasons behind it, which you can find out in the following.

The author writing this book means that, just as some people arrange their rooms, apartments or houses, other people have the right to own venues for video chat, so I can, and I believe I have the right to express my opinion by writing this book about online erotic video chat. I have no intention of upsetting anyone, even if there will be people who disagree about how and why I wrote it and what can happen in video chat; that's why I thought it would be good to protect myself as much as I can to remain anonymous, i.e. not to publish my full name and other personal details about myself.

The book is not written out of desperation to make money, because I have much experience watching video chat models on the internet, or because I want revenge; no way, and about what I wrote in the book,

I didn't intend to report it to make money. The sources where I got the information about erotic video chat are generally from the internet, from my perception and opinions about video chat. At the same time, I read about the abundance of patrons who have video chat studios, searched in the media space, and watched some news about video chat. So, I found out what happens in some video chat studios or what those working in this industry do.

When I first had the idea to write this book, I remember searching the internet for information on video chat and finding nothing but interviews of people working, called video chat models. I listened to conversations of managers about the state of video chat studios, but reasons against online erotic video chat, no. I didn't have an inspiring description of video chat. After that, I started writing what came to my mind, wrote and deleted, wrote and didn't delete and so on, from the first and second pages and moved on. Sometimes, I got stuck and needed help figuring out what else to write; writing the book's structure and connecting the reasons described took me a while.

The book is not intentionally written against people who have a video chat business or against people who work and have a source of income from video chat. Or against people who work for longer than a year doing video chat - I say that because it could be misunderstood as a vendetta against people who do video chat, but it is not written out of revenge.

If you think that the reasons described and the book's content do not justify reason and are not suitable as reasons to make you understand why it is good to give up online video chatting, then please ignore me. I do not claim to be a perfect man, but those working also make mistakes. I want to say why I chose to write these reasons: It is addressed to people who sit on video chat, and if they read what I write here, it may help convince them to stop spending their money and, of course, stop this unhealthy behaviour. The book aims to help some people open their eyes, minds and logic by analysing their beliefs and concluding that time spent repeatedly in front of a laptop, desktop, monitor, or whatever the name may be is time wasted watching models doing video chat. This time spent in front of the monitor, watching people doing a video chat, does not benefit the man's life. Sitting on video chat leads to mentally and physically addictive behaviour. Sitting in front of a monitor, even on the job, watching video chatters, day after day, week after week, month after month or year after year, all lead to chronic and slow pain. You don't die because someone spends time video chatting, but after a while, the body will respond and signal that it's time to do something else, like working a real job, taking care of yourself, or starting a family.

People who frequently video chat are in a family, so they will want to spend as much time with it as possible.

The person working in video chat, a video chat model, is on the other side, in front of a monitor, in a set-up room or outside when the weather is nice. This person has arranged to attract as many people as possible, as many men as possible; I mean men more, because generally, men spend much time after work or during work, or on certain days of the week at the same hours, in front of the monitor to see women almost naked, to see how they move and what they can look like and how they can make them feel sensational. They want to feel that sensation that raises their body temperature, to feel aroused. The person on the other side of the monitor is acting and doing it to make money. Still, it would be best if you found out that person is moving in such a way to attract as many men as possible, and there is probably more than one person watching the same pattern at the same time. The person doing video chat wants to collect as much money as possible; they try to attract those men through different seduction techniques by showing their body or positioning their tour to get more credit and more money. Video chat is a source of income for many people, and couples or married people are working in this field; some people also have children and support their families by doing video chat. The most pleasant and attractive models are young girls who earn pretty well from video chat.

A long time ago, I saw a documentary on TV about prostitution in which a prostitute was asked why she has sex with men for money. She answered that those men *wanted her and asked if men would stop looking for women and paying.*

*for sex, prostitution will stop*. But that will never happen.

Online is different, and you will see why I say that. If men would understand and stop hanging out on video chat, no more people would work as models in set-up studios or from home on online chat sites. Erotic video chat may never stop because they will always be curious, as I was. I remember when I was with a friend, and we watched some pictures online of women in summer lingerie with bras. I also watched it on video chat but didn't pay the money. I admit that I watched on video chat, but very rarely; I may have been on a video chat site in a year, just for a few minutes.

People have different opinions and beliefs, and, for example, many young people have virtual friends that they have not met face to face, have virtual girlfriends that they have not met in real life, and no longer socialise in real life and end up socialising virtually. They transfer their friendship, their love, and their sexuality to the virtual, i.e. it's like they want to be alone, them or them, and nobody physically bothers them any more, through the internet. This shows that video chat sites are in high demand for people who work in studio chat and earn very well; it could be better than that person who watches video chat and pays for that unhealthy desire for satisfaction driven by the fantasy in his head in private. The desires of clients who enter video chat with video chat models show and turn into a dream, and many clients live it and, unconsciously, want that fantasy to stay with them for a while.

# The key to approaching clients on video chat

The presence of models on a video chat website is significant in places specially designed for clients seeking relaxation or satisfaction. Many people who work in video chat try to create a friendly relationship with customers; I call it a hallucinatory relationship because models do not monitor who is watching them; at times, dozens of customers can chat with a video chat model. The relationship created by models working in video chat is to converse, to chat with that man who is alone in his little room and next to him is a bottle or a glass of whatever he prefers to taste. In the client's monitor, who has chosen a video chat model from a video chat website, the video chat model puts himself in front of the client, relates to that man, talks to him, listens to what that man says, makes the atmosphere as relaxed as possible, to be able to create that story between the video chat worker and a temporary client or a potential loyal client.

Models who relate to clients gather experience, know when to speak, and learn when to listen, and clients who write and talk in private will be heard by those who work as models in video chat. Videochat models can also say that they end up like actresses; they have learned the basics because they repeat the exact requirements of the clients, so video chat models do things step by step, forming a specific style of work to attract clients.

The models are usually challenging and will look as natural and friendly as possible to their clients, all to be as appealing as possible. It is possible that, in the beginning, people working in video chat may have made mistakes with first clients and, after a while, learned how to behave and answer questions asked by men. Men find it harder to express their feelings and emotions and talk less than women. Some men end up feeling guilty after some things are done, for example, masturbation. However, they do not understand their guilt; their reason for not changing their desire to sit on video chat is incomprehensible and becomes uncontrollable for men.

Some men don't even think about not going in or watching on video chat, not watching the models, so these people are convinced it's healthy because they're relaxing. For some clients, it's like someone drinking nine beers, and after nine beers, they feel sensational, and then the next day, they realise something is wrong, and they need a beer, but they don't stop at just one. The desire to get on video chat repeats itself. After a short break, even if he feels something is wrong with himself, his misguided perception will not convince him to give up video chat. He continues into the next week or month, i.e. he keeps repeating himself watching video chat even if, after a while, he feels that something is wrong and thinks he should slow down.

Some people frequently enter a video chat website and think they can get into a relationship with one of the video
chat models

The client thinks they may know the video chat model, but more than likely, they don't, and they won't tell them the truth; they may be in a relationship or married. The person who enters video chat thinks that they respect and love themselves, or they need satisfaction, masturbation, not being aware that the satisfaction of watching video chat is fleeting and unsatisfying, that it is a desire to see pleasurable(hedonism) things, beautiful things, arranged women or women who undress for anyone who pays to see them. These girls know that there are men who need to observe naked girls, but the video chat person doesn't ask the client for any completion because she is not sure what is in the client's head.

The time spent on video chat is not seen to be good and beautiful and express happiness for a man because, behind this behaviour of a person's time spent watching models on video chat, there are various reasons or psychological situations such as stressful periods at work if he has a job, lifestyle spent in front of the computer, a computer job. These lead more quickly to the intention to join a video chat website. Many single men enter video chat and prefer young girls. Those who are not young have fewer chances than men who enter a video chat website. Men choose those women who are physically pleasing, so people who work in video chat have set goals and work on techniques to get more clients and earn money.

Adult video chat forums discuss video chatters' opinions, views, ideas, and problems and answer questions. There are guides for video chat models, where those who make mistakes and have different questions are advised and discussed on the forum so that models can better understand how to solve them.

It is easier to deal with difficulties when interacting with customers of video chat websites. It is interesting how it helps some people or some groups of people discuss on adult video chat forums. I assume they do this because of the money. Topics on adult video chat forums focus on attracting customers through music, which must sound excellent and seductive; for example, if a target customer appears on a video chat website, they may be asked: Where is he from? And, if the client answers, then the model will select music according to how they think will have an emotional effect so that the client relaxes and goes private. Even as I write here now, I am not drawn to join a video chat site. I write this way because I wish as few men were entering a video chat website as possible.

Something tells me that what a man does to himself and what he chooses to do with his hand will return to him sooner or later, as he did. If anyone reads these lines and frequents video chat sites, maybe search and enter adult video chat forums. There, he will find interesting discussions between models and video chat managers for training on approaching people who frequent video chat as clients. For example, he would have to understand how he was persuaded to go private because he may have wanted to be personal, but not every time. There are situations where clients feel regret or shame after spending time in private with a video chat model. Why do they think that? Because she did something she didn't intend to do when she first got on video chat. A similar example would be a person who drinks alcohol and talks to someone when they are drunk about what to do to stop drinking alcohol. Interestingly, they wonder what to do to stop drinking alcohol but don't do anything to stop drinking.

# Below, I will present a short discussion I had with a person who has a problem with alcohol and also frequently enters video chat sites and looks at models who do video chat.

After saying that he frequently drinks alcohol and doesn't know what to do to stop drinking, among the discussions, we found out that after he finishes his day job in the evening, he usually drinks alcohol at home and that he has a few girlfriends with whom he chats on a video chat website.

The client is 26 years old. Sex: Male.

**Client**: *In the evening, when I drink beer, I go online and try to chat with models who are on that website on the internet, and I want to continue video chatting. I love girls; I love them with my whole being, their bodies, and how they look.*

**Therapist**: *And is it worth it to consume alcohol and at the same time get into a conversation with models who agree to talk to you?*

**Customer**: *What should I do? If my girlfriend dumped me, I tried to talk to whom I liked; I forgot about the hardships; time passed, and I even went private with a model who does video chat, but it cost me after I went private.*

**Therapist**: *Faced with what you feel when you consume alcohol and go online to models who do video chat and also have a few conversations with those models, do you think it's okay to continue talking to those models in private?*

**Client**: *There's a girl I like, but I can't get her to date me.*

**Therapist**: *So you have a purpose in talking to that girl.*

**Client**: *I want to go and meet her, but I can't.*
I will stop here from replaying what was discussed earlier.

After five months of coming to therapy with interruptions, the client failed to meet that girl and tried to talk to other models but still was unable to meet any of them. He started to enter video chat sites less often to speak to models who do video chat, as well as to understand that drinking alcohol is not suitable for him, and he has days when he does not drink alcohol. This may be short-lived or long-lived in this man's life, whether he gives up alcohol or video chat; I say that because it's up to him what he does in the future.

Suppose anyone is wondering how I came to ask that young man who admitted to watching video chat, from whom I learned about video chat after a few sessions through discussions. In that case, I work as a psychotherapist in my practice. I understand that people who enter video chat as clients lose track of time. Many people who frequently enter a video chat site don't know why it would be good to give up video chat because the satisfaction is misleading. They can't seem to control it; they like to think a certain way and feel that satisfaction. It's like an alcoholic knowing they have alcoholism and wanting to stop drinking but not being able
to control and stop drinking.

# Part II- a

# Definition of the word Reason or reasons

The word "Reason" means the cause of something, justifying something with something else, with an event, an accident, explaining something, to have that reason because of something. Reason or reasoning is a way of thinking in which logic and facts are used; some people use reasoning to decide what is true. From country to country, there may be differences in the description or definition of the word Reason.

## Some examples described as reasons:

The reason I'm asking for your help is that something happened
The police have an excuse to believe he's guilty.

This week, I am still determining his reason for missing work.

Honestly, I don't understand what happened today in my teaching class.

**The following described is in a form that shows several reasons in a description of a particular situation, and the form of the reasons can be understood**

## the logic and knowledge of that person or persons.

He sits on video chat because he's single; he doesn't have a woman. He sits on video chat or wants to sit on video chat even though he is married. It's

He likes video chat, which he wants to chat privately, for which he pays a fee. There would be more to write about the word "Motive", and while searching and reading online, I noticed that the descriptions differ semantically from country to country; I'm referring to countries with an official word definition page.

In the book, the descriptions of reasons on display are not similar or identical, each showing something but not the same thing. So, these motifs are not similar in description, each pointing to something. It isn't straightforward for the mind to understand this behaviour regarding the frequency of presence on video chat, which is convenient, challenging, and very easy to access if you have the internet. Why did I choose to write these reasons? So that men will stop wasting their time on online erotic video ch, below, I will start with an example of a reason to show why it is good not to waste time on online erotic video chats.

## Examples of reasons and, under each reason, a brief description of that written reason.

## For example, If the picture of a woman, attractively arranged, on a video chat site excites you, it may seduce you.

You may be attracted to and seduced by a picture on a video chat site, after which more images and live videos appear for you and seem surprising and appealing, after which you may or almost certainly will want to go further to watch more.

# The first 38 reasons are as follows:

### 1. Online erotic video chat is addictive.

If an addiction to video chat has formed, it can make you give up on yourself because of the women you see on the monitor; through video chat, there is a heightened willingness to make a man masturbate.

## 2. Time spent and wasted on online video chat, repeated daily or weekly, needs to be improved.

Life is short. Try looking to do something useful and avoid getting on video chat to talk to models.

## 3. After a period of video chatting, monitor your screen time.

Make a note at the end of your time in front of the monitor for video chat, even if you might be doing something else besides watching models online.

## 4. A prayer can help if you can't stop sitting in front of the monitor to watch video chat.

Saying a prayer that you think might help you and, over and over again, the same prayer or another prayer so you can stop video chatting and stop looking at those women.

# 5. Strive to find other activities to do instead of sitting in front of the monitor for erotic video chat.

If you're single, you can find a solution that works best for you, such as chatting online with someone to replace watching a video chat.

# 6. Erotic video chat is unhealthy for the human brain.

There is no advantage for a person to having a
      repeated satisfaction watching models doing videos

**7. If you often go on video chat, you may have hormonal and behavioural disorders**

The prolonged and repeated time spent in video chat leads to states of mind and behaviour you are unaware of.

**8. Dopamine is a substance in the brain that can never get enough.**

In short, dopamine is a neurotransmitter in the nervous system. It is a desire, a craving, but not always a pleasure; details about dopamine are in books and on the internet.

**9. Being in a relationship or marrying a woman.**

To live together, love each other and move forward in life,

because people work there, it's a job for some, and some models also have children.

**10. Don't hate models who do erotic video chat.**

Because people are working there, it's a job and

some models also have children; It is just a way to earn money so that they can entertained by video chat.

**11. Don't hurt yourself if you want to stop and can't, so you don't have to sit through online video chat.**

If you've set the goal of getting off online video chat and need to succeed, try to be conscious of your time and slowly close that website.

**12. Models working and preparing to do online and erotic video chat don't look the way they look when they get dolled up through beauty procedures**

That is, they put on foundation and other body and face creams so that the image of those people is very different from reality compared to how they are before they get ready for the video chat.

## 13. If you want to find out what kind of people are models who do erotic online video chat, try to find out.

You can ask if these models want to meet you and find out some details about these people.

## 14. Do you think that models who do online video chat and erotica give out their details about themselves to clients to get to know each other?

Usually, these models work on contract and have partners and friends or are married, but many people are not in a relationship but are just working.

## 15. Models who do erotic video chat do not offer personal details about them to customers.

These models don't like to give details to clients; it's tough to get details about people who do erotic video chats online.

## 16. Some models are forced to work in video chat, and the reality for these people is harsh.

These models may be in situations where they are coerced into online erotic video chat by someone who controls them or is forced to do so because they are in a precarious financial situation or have been persuaded to do video chat, perhaps with promises.

## 17. Professional makeup can be misleading.

Indeed, both the products used and the accessories

clothing is chosen to incite sensual attraction, conveying an illusion, an unreal thing that covers up the clarity and natural expression of a person's image.

**18. It's not worth spending money on erotic video chats.**

Some people find paying for online video chat worthwhile because they have experienced satisfaction.

Still, that satisfaction is momentary, and that desire to feel satisfaction will always need to be stimulated in the imagination of the person seeking that short satisfaction.

## 19. Try to find a video chat studio and see what happens there and what those models do before they go online.

If you're curious, try going to a video chat venue that will show you what happens there.

## 20. Is it worth your honestly earned money to be spent on video chat models?

Wasting your money on this service, thinking it's worth it, wastes both money and time and what you feel is only for the moment. Do you think I will say it's not worth wasting your money? It's your choice what you spend your money on.

## 21. Talk to someone about what you like in an online video chat.

Have you tried talking to someone outside of your friends or family about how you feel about being on online video chat, perhaps a colleague at work or a specialist?

**22. Is online video chat satisfying at the moment, or does it help you over a more extended period?**

Satisfaction is only at that moment, and it remains a reminder that what you did changes your body temperature because it warms you up when you see a nearly naked woman on your monitor.

## 23. In general, shy and withdrawn people are used to sitting on video chat.

Shy guys who discover a female person online get more into video chat; the model on the other side moves for him and smiles at him, which means something sensational, and his senses often lead him to excitement.

## 24. It's not worth it to fantasise about someone you'll only meet online and stick to just talking virtually without serious intention, without ever meeting face to face.

Why would it be worth it to get into a fantasy with someone whose only goal is to make money, but who doesn't directly say they're asking you for money? Think about the fact that you can't touch her, and she's in another country, in front of a monitor, in a room.

## 25. Should masturbation be the main reason you log on to video chat and see someone online and in the right clothes to stimulate you? And is this healthy?

Many female models who are on video chat sites want the client to masturbate to keep longer on private chat. They can't be touched and are in another country, in front of a monitor, in a room.

## 26. Is it okay to fall in love with models you only meet online on video chat and can't meet in person?

It is not good and can lead to depression, and you risk deepening further into loneliness and deep sadness.

## 27. Models who do video chat online want to make life as easy as possible for themselves.

It's a job where they sit in a room, tidy up and wait for the curious to come in. These models are not the kind of people who will support you as a man if you hit the hard times in life or old age.

## 28. The elegance of the clothes used in video chat is a trap.

Usually, the models who do online video chat have stylish clothing, and if you like it and want more, you will see more in private about how they take them off, provided the client pays the model.

## 29. Does a friendship or relationship built by meeting someone through an online video chat site work, and is it possible to bring that person, who might be in another country, to your home?

You may pay a high price and have no guarantee that it will work; you must realise that these models are there for the money. Hope is for everyone, but this means it will happen.

## 30. Do you think models who do online video chat have had a complex or unpleasant financial situation?

You'd better believe it because that's almost certainly why they ended up doing online video chat, but that doesn't mean all people struggling financially do video chat.

## 31. You may want someone who can make more money than you in video chat.

If the model doing video chat had a hard time at first and, after a while, ended up earning considerable money, they may have more money than you, which seems even more interesting to you.

## 32. There is no gain for the person who pays the video chatter. If he is convinced that there is some Gain, then it is from visual illusion, and if you don't like that optical illusion that occurs in that person's mind, it confirms that "*Sight dominates most senses*"!

You're fooling yourself into thinking you're getting something out of paying to see something erotic because you're desperate for a woman. Some women want to get married. Look it up! You may even meet someone to start a relationship with. You may feel content about yourself and the person you could live with.

## 33. With your money, you can do anything and go anywhere; paying models for video chat seems like a good use.

It's not worth throwing your money away on video chat for models in dedicated studios. Even if they claim they don't have a job, these people don't because they don't want just any job, and they are picky. Many models who work in video chat will say that they have had various jobs, but the money needs to be more, and that's true, but you, the one paying, don't care about that. Or are you there to pay for the services of video chat models? For momentary gratification, or brief pleasure, or what reason would there be to spend money on video cha that models?

## 34. In general, models who do video chat do it for several years, and few models have continued to work in video chat for more than ten years.

It's all about the money; that's why these models do video chat. These people discuss and advise each other on how to work and behave in video chat to attract the customers' attention. Some models give up quickly after they start video chatting. Video chatting video chat studios have rules for people working as models. In these studios, experienced people train the models how to work. They are taught how to dress and behave in front of the monitor.

**35. Some video chat studios have rules for people working as models. In these studios, experienced people train the models how to work. They are taught**

**how to dress and behave in front of the monitor.**

These video chat companies have accumulated experience and know how to operate at a particular time of the year. It's like a wheel that turns in a year, and the client is trapped there, watching. That's because there are times during the year when video chat models have more clients.

## 36. Many models working in video chat say this job is their personal development.

What he means by that needs to be clarified. What personal development can someone who moves in front of the monitor to be seen by other people and understand what men want? Customers want satisfaction. They like pleasure; they want to have fun. Does that achieve personal development, or do they know the nature of men and what would suit a particular person, or do they say it to say it?

## 37. Those models who do video chat also have problems; they don't show them, and the issues are masked under the makeup on their faces.

Models who do video chat look lovely, even if they have problems. These problems in the lives of video chat models are not visible, mentally and physically; no sadness or stress is visible on their faces.

**38. All the models who do video chat do it for them. It is an easier job, physically but not mentally.**

The real reason models do video chat is to change their lifestyle and money changes many things in those people's lives, and if they see that they're cashing in, they keep doing it.

# What I think about people who work as models in video chat

You know that video chat models, in general, are women, and these women are used to getting paid for what they look like, for who they are, and once they become video chat models, they want to get as much as they can into their account. You know that the first human being on this earth was a man, then it was a woman. It is described in the reasons, more briefly and directly, why they do and for what these people with the model name do video chat work, and I understand that he, she, or they want to work as a model or models. There would also be why women, throughout their lives, dye their hair different colours, wanting to look further, wanting a change in appearance throughout the stages of life. I know that not all women dye their hair. I understand and believe that people who work as models in video chat studios only hunt for men on the internet if they are looking to get on an adult video chat website. I believe that people who work in video chat don't force anyone to enter it, but as it is written in the middle of the cover as a subtitle, "Sight dominates most senses". These people are there as video chat models because they know that boys or men search online for girls and women, and they search according to the preferences each one has. Men are inclined to look for these kinds of things more.

Like women, it's male; so many men use the internet and choose to spend time with online video chat models, and at the same time, millions of people work as video chat models. With so many people working in video chat to earn money, men spend much time looking at women because they are of almost all nationalities and have a choice. Nearly every model working in video chat finds ways to earn. And what they have to gain is money. A man's addiction to video chat is not visible in reality to the average man. People who work as video chat models will always accept the client or clients as long as they get paid. If someone spends large amounts of money, they will not tell other people because they will be apostrophised for spending their money on the illusion of video chat models.

# The unpleasant life with beautifully groomed models doing video chat

In this chapter, I want to compare the image of a person as a video chat model and her image arranged for clients, in antithesis to the picture of the same person agreed but not as a video chat model. The effect of cosmetics on the skin and hair used by a person on a video chat website is very misleading and false. One person who worked as a model I saw by chance from another country was from the city I was from. I noticed her as a model on a video chat website while living and working in another country. I worked for 14 years in London, and after a while, I returned to my hometown, where the person from that video chat site also lived. I noticed that person in real life on the street. I didn't recognise her when I first looked at her, but I wondered how I knew her. In reality, she looked completely different in physiognomy and hair on the street, in a way you wouldn't think of dealing with that person. The people who hire models who do video chat have specialised approaching and recruiting agencies, have experience and train the models, teaching them how to behave.

I wrote something similar on other pages about managers who train models for video chat.

In reality, the lives of clients who watch models doing video chat are no better. Some so many people have access to the internet but don't log on to a video chat site to protect models. At the same time, models are taking advantage of the beauty industry, which is developing innovations in aesthetics and becoming loyal to consistent consumers. The science of aesthetics is addressing different personalities who, using beauty products made of mixed chemicals, have now become more conscious and are switching to natural beauty products, using mixtures with natural oils, so that these products are more varied and beneficial, more advanced but more expensive, and give a much different look, at the moment. They probably use vitamins in these creams, oils, and face masks, which benefit the skin.

I believe that a beautiful woman is a woman who wears herself naturally, that is, without foundation, manicure, pedicure or whatever. Women, in their naturalness, are more beautiful. On video chat, you will find a few models who look natural; they seem to use a lot of body and face creams. I don't understand the satisfaction of men watching women with a layer of almost a half-millimetre thick foundation on their face, dyed hair, and maybe wearing a wig; they also have false eyebrows dressed in attractive lingerie or clothes that attract men's eyes. I'm not against models working in a video chat studio or people who have a video chat business or make a living, but I wouldn't say I like foundation masks on a woman's face that cover up that person's true face. I worked outside a hair salon for a year, and every girl and woman would walk past my apartment for a while.

I wondered where these women go every day. I expected to notice fewer girls and women going to the hair salon, which was very crowded. That salon, having hours until 8 p.m., made appointments for clients by phone. I learned this from my cousin, who lived in the area and went to that hair salon. Throughout life, women want to have a hair colour change. I'm not trying to criticise people who go to the hairdresser because if they go to the hairdresser once, they can learn and do their hair while they can.

## The following 39 reasons are described.

**39. If you've been on video chat and think you'll meet someone who works in a video chat studio or from home, you should know that chances are slim that you'll meet physically or in person.**

Models who work on video chat don't usually go to meetings with their clients because they don't accept clients from their area; they need to know if a client has ever actually talked to people who do video chat.

## 40. Long periods, even years, looking at video chat models can lead to chronic problems with a slow progression.

The real reasons you watch video chat are your feelings and desires; something is wrong. You can learn more about what that means if you want information from a specialist.

## 41. It's better to spend time with your girlfriend or find a girlfriend if you don't have one.

Having a girlfriend in the future may lead to a relationship and perhaps further to marriage and family.

## 42. At certain times of the day, the impulse that urges you to go to a video chat website is fundamental to be aware of to understand in what situations that desire to get on video chat happens to occur.

There are times during the day or in the evening when a person is doing something that has nothing to do with the models doing video chat, and they happen, after a short time, to get on video chat to talk to the models. When that impulse comes, it is motivated by something specific inside the body and the head. Sometimes, people who get on video chat can say they need to observe those models doing video chat.

## 43. Some models who do video chat and work every day think about the people who pay to watch video chat, that they are not sane, and that they have some psychological problems.

I believe this because I heard from someone with experience who said that it would be better not to go overboard with the information given to clients about models working in video chat, not to reveal their identity, because there are clients who ask models to look at absurd things, such as wanting to see their toes, and the approach is a strange one.

## 44. Loyalty and faithfulness for video chat models are psychological dispositions.

Loyal customers of video chat models are generally men who are more reluctant to meet a woman in person. However, they are still open about other things, such as earning money at work or in business.

**45. To be attracted to something you can't have is to suffer, not to understand yourself; what you want through video chat you can't have, and you almost certainly will never have that person, but you continue to stay on video chat.**

There are many situations where many men have sexual desires and fantasise about going on video chat, asking to see things they wouldn't ask their wife or girlfriend. The human mind has a rich imagination, so it's good to understand, step by step, what's going on with you and, if you want, seek a specialist or a psychologist who can help you.

**46. Your passion and obsession with watching models doing video chat and spending money can lead to an addiction that risks controlling you, like gambling; i.e. the addiction within you stems you mentally and physically, your internal resistance to the addiction is overcome, and so the addiction is built.**

Maybe you realise that addiction can hurt you, i.e. damage your soul, or perhaps you don't even care. You end up saying, "The important thing is to feel good now because life is short, and I don't know what tomorrow will bring", and take the opportunity to do those things that satisfy you.

**47. Models working on video chat sites don't care about your money; they want to earn as**

## much as possible.

Watch your money because things can change in the future since you're throwing money at people who do video chat.

## 48. Video chat can capture and shackle your curiosity for a living.

Models working in video chat studios feel how things work with their clients and create a relationship with them through video chat. It sounds strange, but it Is true. In this relationship, people who work in video chat have learned how to behave and feel how clients are and what they want. Models create relationships with clients to lure them into private, where they must pay.

## 49. Understanding that it's unhealthy to spend money on video chat is a step towards your well-being.

Your time and your life are much more important than models doing video chat; even if you don't know what else you could be doing, if you understand, it's necessary to do something to quit video chat.

## 50. Sometimes, it is a joy to see some clients' favourite models working on the chat or a specific model pleasing the client.

It's less accurate than you think it is to go private with someone who only does it for money with you and other clients. At the end of the program, these models who do video chat go home to their husbands and children, if married, and don't go private with just one client. Where do you think she makes $40K in a month?

## 51. People who spend time with video chat models don't understand that they are missing out on natural love.

Touching yourself alone or alone and masturbating is not true love; some may say, "Well, I touch myself, but I don't masturbate".

## 52. How you live might be what you like, what satisfies you, but it's always only for a certain period. Have you wondered where you'll end up if you keep talking to models who do video chat?

Clients who are used to getting into video chat are left with the satisfaction and pleasure of the moment, and there is little chance for clients who think they can physically meet models doing video chat.

## 53. Try doing something else with that money you're considering spending on video chat! Donate to a hospital or someone who helps people!

The feeling of donating a sum of money to someone who is helping sick people can mean more and be more satisfying than the feeling and excitement you get when you are privately video chatting. Emotions and feelings are not the same things, but they work together.

## 54. If the picture of an attractive woman attracts you, it doesn't mean that picture is for you.

Often, a picture says a lot and gives much meaning, but only some clients will fall for that picture on a video chat website.

## 55. Models who work on video chat work hard to earn money because they realise that this is the time for them and that it can't last long to pursue this profession.

In video chat studios, people who work gather and talk to each other and know that now is the time to pull out all the stops and do what they can to make money from clients.

## 56. It needs to be corrected if you think that no one will find out that you watch video chat, have spent your money, and can do whatever you want with your money. Why do I say that? Because you may be giving yourself away.

Sometimes, a man tells the truth about his life and often speaks about some things. We are hidden with a stranger rather than with a family member or friend.

## 57. Are you sure you're not fooled by what you see on your monitor or watching a video chat site because of your emotional desire? Do you think it's worth it? And until when?

People who work as video chat models are there to attract clients, and you are there because there is something wrong with you, even if you don't believe or understand that you are missing someone physically with you.

## 58. What does it help to have masturbation in a particular place? What motivates you? Does it

## make you feel different?

It solves absolutely nothing to get aroused looking at women; it does nothing for you. You're cheating yourself. Some doctors say that ejaculation relaxes the body. I'm afraid I have to disagree that a man should frequently masturbate.

## 59. Here's something about men who want to have as many women as possible that they don't actually have and are trying, online, to spend wasted and misunderstood time.

Men want to have as many children as possible, but they want someone to take care of those children because when they are heading towards old age and death, they want

to have more children.

## 60. Men are not very good at expressing their emotions in words, which sometimes leads to vulnerable behaviour, but a man's happiness is not in a woman's hand but in freedom and soul love with a soul mate and not with models.

Men talk less than women; by nature, they are focused on practical functions, getting things done, and acting more than women. That's why many men search and talk to women on online dating platforms and video chat websites.

## 61. The youth is not aware that they will regret it later. Towards the end of life, more regrets come into the man's mind just as the desire to enter video chat comes.

Regrets come after a certain age, and living with them in old age is hard. Trying to understand the routine of sitting on video chat doesn't help you; old age will be more complex and full of regrets.

## 62. The critical moment of relapsing into wanting to be on video chat is to be aware of yourself and realise that it is the most important.

When the desire to sit on video chat comes, it automatically activates the prevention of your falling and relapsing into that urge you feel as a desire in your body, which comes in the form of pleasure-seeking. Understand that moment at the beginning, when you enter a video chat site and realise that it's not good to go there and that at the root is an impulse that has arisen uncontrollably but that you can control by becoming aware of it and repressing it.

## 63. If you get into a long-distance relationship with a model through video chat, it is cold, unlike a real-life relationship and physical contact.

As a client, if you happen to meet someone online and chat for a long time, for months, without a meeting, and after a while, you wish it would come to the time of the meeting, chances are very high that it will be a failure, that you won't be able to meet the model who does video chat. Some models have said in their interviews that they are men. I asked them to meet, but they refused, finding reasons not to meet physically.

## 64. Doing this for a long time and watching models doing video chat can make people's minds feel like they're in a fantasy room.

In the minds of those people who often enter video chat sites, imaginary but failed relationships are frequently created. Many keep going, looking to chat with models who work in video chat.

## 65. Why is it kept hidden that talking to video chat models is harmful? To convince you that it's okay to masturbate?

What is the feeling of satisfaction when masturbating? In my opinion, it is wrong, undeserving and wrong that masturbation should be understood as a form of relaxation or stress relief. Ejaculation has its senses because when a man ejaculates, the body has other sensations more distinct from the other human senses, and relaxation of the body can be achieved in different ways.

## 66. Shame and pride, if they are correlated, might have the same meaning.

Did you know that nine out of ten people working on video chat did not tell where they worked and hid from the beginning? After earning considerable money, they bought cars, apartments, and houses, and now they no longer care what is said about the models who do video chat. Do you know why? They are richer because of men who don't understand their impulses, repeatedly keeping up the pace of satisfaction.

## 67. Video chat deceives your senses - it tricks your instincts.

Someone said it's not so easy not to get on video chat. I mean, the impulse in my head automatically went to making me think I was having a good time and that reasonable time for someone meant pleasure, and I would describe that satisfaction as mind-blowing.

## 68. People who work in video chat only care about their clients if they pay. They want to create a relationship with the client and pretend to be dedicated to the client, but they are there for the money, so they work as models in video chat.

Money is the main reason for being on video chat, but to get that money from video chat studios, the models get specific instruction, become trained - or self-trained - and learn how to convince you that video chat is worth watching. Someone pays, and someone gets paid.

## 69. Is it worth masturbating because you see a woman on a monitor from who knows what country? Even if she's not near you and looks to your liking, she's there to satisfy your needs.

One of the reasons for masturbation in men is loneliness and lack of socialisation. If you have no friends and no one to socialise with, that means you need socialisation, or even if you do have conversations, you still masturbate at some point in your life, but that doesn't mean all men are the same.

## 70. What is behind the uncontrolled desire? You believe that it would be good to sit on video chat and watch pussy!

Close the video chat page, and don't open it again. Quit to something like this before you waste time or lose your nerve!

## 71. Love is a video chat play. But love has meaning and its way of working. Real love is NOT through video chat!

Love is life, God-given in People, but love by video chatting, seeking satisfaction, throwing your seed on the ground, or something else is vanity.

# 72. Sometimes, they get on video chat and from how the conversation goes, they think there's a possibility of a long-distance and normal relationship.

You're almost certainly deluding yourself into thinking you can end up with someone in a video chat in a healthy, future-proof relationship. Many people move their socialising, friendships, relationships and love online, which could be better.

# 73. Videochat has become an industry, a money-making machine.

For some people, it's heaven; for others, video chat is harmful. Videochat has its good and not-so-good sides.

# 74. For example, you can also try self-conviction work: "I stopped going online to look at the model or models doing video chat."

It's a good idea and would be a good fact and a change in the life of that person who will no longer go in to watch models working on a site, or several sites simultaneously, video chatting.

# 75. If there are problems in the life of that person who goes to watch Girls on a video chat site, it doesn't mean that there, in private, the issues are solved.

That doesn't mean that if people have problems, they need to sit on video chat and relax and forget about the concerns, or they will solve themselves. Video chat doesn't solve problems; it's like an ejaculation, which many men do to feel good, but it doesn't solve emotional issues.

## 76. People working in video chat are always willing to provide emotional and physical satisfaction for their clients.

It is well-known why video chat models pay attention to clients, who are generally men because almost all clients who enter video chat want to feel pleasure and satisfaction.

**77. It's just in your heart and mind to want to get on video chat, and once you think of happiness, there's no more desire to stay on video chat. Remember that you are also dragging your soul after these fleeting desires.**

If you know from the beginning that it is good to stop entering a video chat site, you will manage to stop searching and entering to see those models who do video chat.

## Aspects of the reasons described

These reasons generally relate to people who are frequent or long-time users of multiple video chat sites or who are just starting and want to watch video chat models, but also to people who are unhappy with the time they spend and what they do in private with video chat models. Some people have regrets after spending some time on video chat, but they can't understand in-depth, and they can't set a goal to reduce or replace the time spent online on video chat. Or, after a while, someone will think and believe that they will give up on themselves to stop watching models on video chat and that they will reach saturation and perhaps never enter again. I would ask someone who frequently enters a video chat site: do they think giving time and money because of the desire to watch video chatter will bring them healthy satisfaction? Perhaps they would answer yes, no or don't know. It is satisfying if it pays off in money, but what are you giving away through video chat? A sum of money. And is that money worth throwing out because sight dominates the human senses? Or may the money you give be returned to you by someone from another country who shows their body for money? But what else are you giving away in your life: your time, your feelings of love, the attention you should

To give it to your family, if you have a family. Doesn't the habit of spending time on video chat because you need a partner? Or are there other reasons?

When a man ejaculates, he does it for himself to feel different from how he handles the rest of the day. But in his heart, does he want to spend his time watching models online on video chat? I sit and wonder, what is the satisfaction for a man to watch models who are there to make money? The fulfilment is because he doesn't realise that he's stuck in a fantasy or gets to live in an imaginary world.

Someone said that money comes easy and goes fast. I don't know if that's true, but it may be as that someone or more said. People from other countries and different cultures seem to be more attractive to most men, which leads them to seek out and look at more women from different parts of the earth. For example, in England, black men, but I don't mean all black men, look for Caucasian women; so do many women who want to live and have a family with men who have a different skin colour from their partner. If a man from Africa, having the colour of African people, and a woman from Europe, having white skin, try to conceive a child and have a child, the colour of that child's skin will be more exciting and pleasing to the eye. I discovered that people who do video chat and are in one area of a country can choose the nations from which they accept clients. For example, if the person doing the video chat is from Ukraine, they will not have people who have access to their IDs, and not only from Ukraine, but they can also be from neighbouring countries around the country they are in. I have heard that most models who do video chat prefer to get clients from the US,

Canada, Australia, the UK, and France because the earning level is higher, and they probably make more time for online video chat.

People who focus on online work form a belief about things differently than people who talk to people in real life and do physical work, who work more without a phone and ignore internet access. I have an example of a comparison between myself and the person who called me today as I write this. One day, I placed an ad that I was renting an apartment, and after the ad was placed, among other people asking about the apartment, I had a conversation with someone looking for another place to live. In my talk, he told me that he was working from home and, in paying the rent, asked me if he could do it by bank transfer. After a discussion of about three minutes, this person told me that I was not of the nationality of the country I was in and that I was a foreigner, even saying that she was sure that I was a foreigner. I said I could show her an ID but ended the discussion. I'm passing here about this discussion related to his conviction as a man who works online and from home, and that is that this man was convinced that I am a foreigner by the way I speak, even if it is not as he says.

I thought about myself, the way I speak and express myself, or his thinking may mislead him because he works from home and only online, and thus be misled because he has a different perception of reality. And then I ask myself: why a person who frequents online models on video chat does not realise and think about the consequences that will come later and that he does not feel in those days and thus may end up having health problems? Clients who often enter video chat need help finding it.

understand, or even care at those times, if they know that video chat brings them emotional and sentimental satisfaction and that they need to see or watch people on video chat.

Clients who spend much time on video chat do not perceive any harm in their actions. On the contrary, they think they or they believe it is a good thing and worth staying on video chat. They don't see anything disturbing or unpleasant. So make sure it's not too late when you realise that something is wrong with you, and you can't fix the damage done to your psyche, ending up having to undergo treatment or medication. If anyone wonders what can happen if you stay a long time on video chat, I wrote in the reasons described.

# Part III- a

## What's behind this desire to enjoy video chatting

If one would like to identify and clarify the assessment of the condition that would seem not to be a problem and what is causing some people to enter a video chat site and chat with models there, and if an assessment of the issue is desired, there is a method of psychological or therapeutic counselling. If they tried, they would understand that it is necessary to overcome their emotional problems related to practical issues, such as being eager to be satisfied through video chat on online models, which leads to masturbation and seminal ejaculation. This would be one of the factors why he feels the desire to get on video chat, even if before getting on video chat, he does not think about ejaculation, but as he looks at a model, he cannot control himself.

It's up to the person to choose whether they talk to someone about their behaviour. People who enter and stay on video chat for a long time do not speak to anyone else to hear an opinion about video chat that would make them stop the behaviour. In men, love and romance are the necessary factors in arousing the desire to search, with men being inclined to explore more than women, and need to satisfy themselves. On the female side, those who pay men who do video chat are a minimal number compared to men who pay women who do video chat. A strange and straightforward thing would be self-love or love for someone. The two are not in conflict, but self-love, for example, can show that you love the child in you, and love for someone is great when you love the woman who needs love or when you love the man in you who needs freedom. I write in this way about self-love because so many men masturbate, starting with the first signs by touching their bodies.

These loves may be compatible with love for others, but if you love, it shows that you love yourself, too. How you love yourself online leads to an unhealthy habit and is not felt as, in reality, it is not natural, like that feeling of love when you touch and physically live with someone. The love in you defends you from harm, but you are still the person who takes it to the other extreme.

This little book may make you feel frustrated and dissatisfied with what you've read if you're a single person who works online from home and video chats a lot. It may give you a feeling of insecurity about video chat, and I probably haven't written everything; maybe I have left many things out, but I think it's enough what I have written because I do not believe all books are read from the beginning to end and that's why this little book is not many pages just to be noted here.

What you might feel or understand about what I've written here: you might think that it can't be a bad idea to stop video chatting or chatting only occasionally, thinking it's no big deal. But so has anyone who has gone from fun to gambling addiction or from a drink to alcohol addiction.

You Started with curiosity. The beginning was easy; it started with a game of gambling or a drink with some alcohol in it, and after that, only they know what they would do next, which is why even virtual video chat for adults is very enjoyable for many people since it is accessed by millions of users monthly. You may feel embarrassed to talk to someone about video chat. Still, if you want to continue to watch women on video chat and spend money, it would be good, at least after a while, to calculate your expenses and time spent, as well as your satisfaction that you felt aroused; I say aroused because after all there is the intention, to reach satisfaction. You don't need that kind of excitement on a daily, weekly, or more extended-period basis.

Someone said that adult video chat is an industry that prevents male suicide. And I can say that the necessary body food is part of a person's life to protect him from starvation, disease and death! But they are different from the video chat industry and human food.

Adult webcam has become an industry, but it doesn't keep men from committing suicide. Why do I say that? Because a person's behaviour of sitting on the webcam is hallucinatory, it's covert thoughts in his mind that appear instantly; they are influenced all by that body, i.e. he doesn't understand exactly why those thoughts appear instantly in his head and lead him to improper, delusional behaviour. I say illusory because watching video chat, especially at night, leads to misperception, generating exaggerated sensations and pleasures. If he doesn't understand why those thoughts arise in his mind, he believes he needs to do that thing sitting on video chat to watch models. But what happens when he thinks about not sitting on video chat?

She can't stop herself from going on video chat, so she follows her impulse and thoughts to go on video chat. And where does it end up?

Everything ends, sooner or later, for better or worse. It is just as death is part of life; the fact that we are born determines the fact that we will die. You can never get back the time spent on video chat, but looking at something enjoyable and worth spending that money on for many people is not regrettable. I have known and know a few kinds of people who are alcohol addicts and keep their jobs. They go to work every day, but after work, they drink alcohol almost every day. I have observed a few people, both on and off the job, who are addicted to alcohol but who are also very serious and focused on the work they have. What surprises me, and I have often wondered, is why, after they finish their work hours, they go out and consume alcohol daily. That's what I could say about video chat, too; why does a man need to watch and go in private with models doing video chat? If anyone is reading, they can say: Well, you asked, and you still answered. The answer differs from person to person because everyone is different and unique in their way. Everyone has personal or less personal reasons for joining a video chat site. There would also be the desire of the men who enter video chat to feel that they please the model doing the video chat, that they are doing what is asked of them because the clients feel that they initiated that pleasure. That pleasure they become addicted to seeing through video chat results from the video chat model transferring money into their account or earning points.

# Sigth dominates most senses.

Feeling that something is wanted leads to seeking and visualising, so the mind works with the image that the eyes transmit to the brain through what it sees. The mind and the senses in the body want something to feel good. Related to video chat, people who get into conversations with models who do video chat need to notice to see, which makes them even more determined to go forward. Some people say that the eyes mirror our soul, and they mean how those eyes reflect the person's being. The impulse and desire to see models groomed and ready for video chat instantly appear in the human body, and models in video chat are like actors who have something to do; they're prepared for what's next if someone pays them. Models who do video chat have learned how to groom themselves, talk or have a pleasing appearance for people who look for women through video chat. The presence of the models induces the mood and conviction that it is worthwhile to sit on the video chat, to look at living human beings and desire the sensation of pleasure because of the watching eyes. The visual illusion has to do with the mind of the person used to enter a video chat site. An illusion is a misperception of an existing sensation about something. Illusion shows a change of senses, often done intentionally. This means that some people are convinced.

It's worth watching on video chat, even if they must realise that they are fooling themselves by what they observe and choose to watch on video chat because it's a waste of time. The desire to see people offering services through video chat comes back; it is in the person's beliefs to want to be on video chat, and what they feel is a desire that has a little end, that is, that desire to get on video chat is repeated. Giving up video chat requires changing some habits in behaviour to understand that watching video chat very often is time wasted.

With the eyes, man sees, learns and understands the things around him. An adult looks with his eyes at healthy or unhealthy things for his mind and body. A man can be motivated and influenced to do certain things by what he sees and convinces him that it is right to do that thing. For example, a picture is as long as ten written pages for many people. Depending on what that picture looks like, it will give meaning and lead to conviction to decide. I connect with people who watch video chat models, and it's known what models do in video chat. One can stop watching if there is the courage to stop watching, even if the body demands it.

# Some questions I asked myself when I was writing the book:

## Some of the questions were not attractive, but they were positive in a good way.

Why do men need to pay online to watch a woman's pussy while far too few women pay for a man's toy?

What is in the mind of that unsatisfied person if they keep getting the urge to get on video chat?

Is there anything else that can seduce you and get you hooked? It could be the clandestine thoughts that instantly appear, along with the body's senses, stimuli from the brain, from the person's subconscious and memory, if he keeps repeating the desire to sit on video chat, or owns too much money and is not sure how to spend it.

What does a man think of models on video chat and working there?

Would you like to meet your future wife by completing her as a model working in video chat? It's possible, yes. Are there many men who want to marry girls who work as models in video chat studios? Are there men married to wives who work in video chat? Yes, some men have

Wives are working as models in video chat studios or from home.

What can someone do when they realise they are on video chat and know it's not right but can't quit? Can't they close that video chat page? I'm talking about the person who is used to being on video chat.

How can a man explain the satisfaction he's had, created by someone on the monitor? Is this healthy?

Men and women cannot be equal. Each has a different role in life.

Why is a man charmed or attracted to video chat?

The client, after he finds that person and has done what he felt after he's done with the money and watching video chat, what does he want?

# It can lead to a form of video chat addiction, on video chat

## Models?

The terms addiction or dependence are similar, but I have chosen to write the word addiction. It can happen to anyone who enters a video chat website to become addicted. At first, entering out of curiosity, pleasure, or fun on video chat, it seems pleasant to see a human being on your or someone else's monitor. I frequently use the idea that addiction has been reached from video chat or has been reached because of erotic video chat. To get addicted to video chat, a few factors cause those people to feel attracted to or are influenced by other people around them, and I'm talking about boys and men because they are the first ones to enter a video chat site. There are also women and older people, and some of these people who enter a video chat site end up being addicted; that is, they enter frequently and seek pleasure or some satisfaction that they need pretty often.

Suppose a person goes in almost daily or weekly to watch people who do video chat after a few months. In that case, they seem to lean towards other ideas, move on, change their desire to feel pleasure and start looking for people from a different culture, with a different physical appearance, and from other age groups. The behaviour of an addicted person via video chat is like a wheel; his behaviour rolls in his searches over one year.

He happens to come in one day or several days, one after the other, for a few hours, then takes a break for a few days, then comes back and comes in to watch video chat models again. After a more extended period than a year, he enters a video chat site even if he is not aware that, after a year, he has built an addiction due to his repeated behaviour and spent in front of the monitor watching video chat models. Many people are not aware that they have an addiction formed from entering a particular video chat site. Still, the addiction that makes them enter to watch the models leads to a desire to feel good and experience pleasure. In a comparison between alcohol addiction and addiction to video chat models, it is not the perception of the same feeling or emotion. Being on a video chat site makes it feel good and forget about the necessary human things in a man's life, thanks to the models who, if paid, behave as the client wants in their specially designed room. The mind and behaviour of the person addicted to video chat are cut off from reality. It can lead to a form of addiction because of video chatting, and that can be very damaging in the long run. The person's mind and behaviour become like a lid, and they are unaware of the consequences of their addiction even if they say they are in an addiction because of people who video chat. In one article, I read about video chat addiction that can lead to depression, panic attacks, anxiety, obsessive-compulsive behaviour, frigidity, destabilisation of relationships and marriages, and even divorce and family arguments. Life is not beautiful or pleasant when a person is in a form of addiction or has.

Addictive behaviour for something. Everything is an illusion or fantasy in the minds of those who are addicted. Consuming an unhealthy substance or engaging in harmful behaviour is like some people believing that life is meaningless or that there is no God. There are people who, because of addictive behaviour or having addictions to substances or alcohol, have committed suicide. Why do I think some people are addicted to models who video chat for gratification? Because many people come into video chat early in the day, during the day, evenings, and nights, it has become routine for many. How do I know people come in during the 24 hours to video chat? Because on video chat sites, the models are on 24/7. I heard about her work schedule in an interview with a person who worked as a model in a video chat studio. It started at 06:00 in the morning in the country where she lived, and the models were

selected by rotation.

# How to be aware of your time

## when you are online, on video chat

I've also written in the form of questions, and I know many questions are being asked, and some may get attention. If the questions are interesting, write them down on paper and write your answer under each question. Do you know what you want online or your expectations of video chat models? Or does a thought cross your mind and let's go online and watch those cute girls, or do I go online out of curiosity or habit on a video chat site? What exactly happened to you that you ended up joining video chat alone and of your own free will? These questions are addressed to men who generally enter a video chat site, and the answer would be the possibility of finding yourself in one or more of the reasons described above. Can they find out what happened to themselves before they entered video chat so they don't repeat that desire and impulse? What thoughts come to mind? If you want to stop video chatting, ask yourself what you can do before you go online and when you are on video chat. What are the expectations while you are on virtual chat, and how do you feel after watching on video chat? Or, if you fail to understand the impulses that lead you to a video chat site, you may think or wonder.

Next: Why were you born? Why are you growing up? Why do you go to school? Why are you learning new things? And why, as an adult, do you choose to do some unhealthy stuff? What is the satisfaction of sitting on video chat? If you can answer these questions, you can identify why you can't stop video chatting. Do they have the same thoughts or desires when joining a video chat site? Or are they no longer thoughts or desires, but perhaps was an automatic, suddenly activated impulse from the brain that came to you, and you joined a favourite video chat site, after which sight dominates all the senses? Is life beautiful when the mind is unconsciously doing unhealthy things?

When a man is chatting, a desire demands satisfaction during the interaction. Is he convinced that he needs that satisfaction, and is it okay to pay money to see a naked woman online? Because he is in his room and no longer wants to move physically, is it better to sit quietly to do what he wants, and how does he want to go online to a video chat site? Surely the man needs this satisfaction of sitting on the video chat for days, weeks, months, maybe even years? I wrote days and months, but I don't mean daily or every day. It can be a period when entering video chat, where days repeat one after the other watching video chat or maybe even months. After a person has been on video chat, one can think about what he feels, how he feels or what he thinks. In the end, is there still that desire to look at the models as before they went on the video chat when they first thought about it? Or did he feel about going in and watching the girls or whoever was there in the chat out of curiosity to pass the time? Or chatting to someone because it helps to have a conversation with someone? In a discussion between a man and a woman about sex, the woman knows that after a man ejaculates, the sexual act is over.

And models who do video chat know that if the client goes private, they want satisfaction but may need to notice it.

One day, I was in a room with several people, and someone asked me if I smoked. I replied that I didn't smoke and that I was a non-smoker. We kept talking, and everyone was doing their own thing, and the person who asked me if I smoked and to whom I replied that I was a non-smoker told me that it was good that I didn't smoke. I noticed that he was comparing and meant that he would like to quit smoking but couldn't. He may have tried to quit smoking, but he can't stop. Every smoker who says don't smoke has their reasons for saying so. Regular alcohol drinker who has an addiction to alcohol does not recommend young people to drink alcohol. There are people with alcohol addiction, and if they have discussions with young people who consume alcohol, they sometimes tell young people to give up alcohol; that is, the soul of that person means that it is not good to consume alcohol. But about video chat, they don't talk or tell pro and con opinions by people who frequent video chat. Few people come in and talk to models who do video chat since it has become an industry, and millions interact with models who do video chat.

# Part IV- a

## The curiosity of young people under 20 on video chat

Guys are generally curious to get on video chat sites and watch the models. They're curious about girls' bodies and what their bodies look like. Boys talk and interact less with girls; more and more boys use the internet, and through it, they go further in finding out intimate things about girls. Surfing the internet, from a simple picture, they can end up on a webchat site, which is very easy to access and view. From there, I started to search and find out more about girls. Some boys begin with a touch of their sexual organs, and in many cases, after a while, it leads to masturbation and after a time, they realise that they can't control themselves anymore, that is, even if they are at home and they are with the family. There are family members in the house, and that boy finds a place to masturbate, maybe in the bathroom or at night in bed. It seems that this desire in boys to masturbate is related to feeling, and what they feel is different from other senses; it is assimilated into the sensation of pleasure. In reality, these boys who masturbate will not open topics by saying that they do it because it is shameful and unpleasant, but end up after a while not being able to control themselves and continue to

Masturbate frequently. With their minds and senses driven by the desire to masturbate, many guys take online video chat to stimulate themselves by looking at models. Often, during masturbation, they need to notice something pleasurable or imagine something pleasant. Interestingly, although guys have preferences and, choosing from girls on the internet, find a pleasing person to look at and masturbate to, there are many situations when they masturbate and are not on video chat, ending up imagining a model they have seen and thought looked good. It seems that after a while, many guys want to stop watching on video chat, and sometimes they can't. Over time, the frequency on the internet and looking at girls becomes more and more and ends up being a habit or a form of addiction, which is not healthy; it is harmful to the psyche and the human body.

The definition of addiction can be found in books or on the internet, and I am not defining it here because I am not trying to convince anyone that this is the definition of the word "addiction". You can easily find out what addiction is from a web page.

# Men doing video chat.

The number of men doing video chat has increased since the Coronavirus Pandemic. During the pandemic, video chat was model gold. People were forced to work from home. Then, the number of men doing video chat increased, and many continue to make a living from video chat. Searching on the internet about men doing video chat, I generally found information and explanations from video chat studios having specialised websites and the possibility of approaching men who want to become video chat models. Are men successful in erotic video chat? Yes, they do and probably earn well. I've noticed in this industry that on some video chat sites, there are criteria by gender categories, where there are single men or gay couples, which means that most men who do video chat have work. Many people are interested in male models, not only female models, and what they do there in video chat is only what they know. I read in an article that a man who does video chat managed to pay off all his bank payments for the next five years and recently bought a luxury car. I won't say where it says it because it's not true, but I state it because the article's appearance seems to be a way to attract boys and men to video chat.

# Willingness to change their time spent on video chat

It's just the intention to change something about his beliefs on online video chat, and only if he wants to give up on staying on video chat, it's a start, but it depends on which direction he wants to change. I will write about changing the person to give up video chat, and he can start by looking in the mirror and saying, "I'm going to start changing". If you're in front of a mirror and say that, try to figure out how or what you feel. Why do I say try to understand how you think? People can change if they know their emotional and feeling states towards what they're doing, and if you're here and you're reading this book, it means you want to change something, and there's a problem in your behaviour about how often you're on and how long you're on video chat. A person doesn't solve their state problem on video chat because they are emotionally affected by the issues weighing them down. They can't stop watching video chat online, which is relaxing. Suppose she realises that underlying her behaviour are the emotional states that influence her behaviour. In that case, she can understand and identify her feelings while on video chat and remember them. It can be an emotion, which is sometimes healthy or unhealthy. I will present two examples of emotions: rational and irrational. I also call them healthy emotions and unhealthy emotions.

## Two examples of emotions:

**Personal judgement Healthy Emotion** and **Unhealthy Emotion**

Personal weaknesses  Regret            Shame

Breaking rules        Dissatisfaction   Furies
staff

If anyone is wondering what emotion they can feel when on video chat, it's what they think before they get on video chat; that impulse leads them to get on a video chat or adult site. But suppose they can't identify what they're feeling. In that case, they can think about, when they thought about getting on video chat, what mental, physical and emotional state they were in when they thought about getting on video chat because there are some factors around that can influence a person's beliefs, making them think it's okay to do that. He wants to feel good watching a video chat site because he wants pleasure and satisfaction. In short, many people are emotionally affected by what they perceive happening around them. Namely, the inner desire to be on video chat leads to pleasure and satisfaction. The change in the urge to watch video chat does not come by itself, but over time, it can diminish or amplify; one can give up video chat willingly for many reasons (lack of money) or join a video chat site daily or weekly (I need, I like that person). If your will is weak, you have no self-confidence because you can't control yourself—those who stay on the video chat for a long time can choose to quit. The person who frequently enters a video chat site to watch those models is the only person who can change the impulse, thinking and behaviour to stop entering a video chat site to look at those models.

That person who frequently goes on video chat, if they expect someone or somewhere to do something to change, then it's not going to happen, and they don't care; they don't want to change. I'll give an example of someone who wants to understand change but does nothing. This is the same as when the wife brings her husband to the cabinet because of game addiction. After the session at the cabinet has started, within the first ten minutes, the man in the cabinet answers questions with "I don't know". Videochatters don't want to try not to stay on video chat; it won't solve anything, but if, at first, he's curious to get off video chat, like somewhat interested in getting on video chat, got addicted curiosity and want to look at those models and ends up masturbating and feels it's not right, then work against the decisions made when he gets on. Or it's on video chat to understand that they have to and convince themselves that it's worth it to give it up; it sounds wild, but it is. For example, some people say they are drinking alcohol for the last time, and the next day, when they drink, they will say the same. You have to work step by step to give up video chat or a possible video chat addiction. It will be a struggle with self that takes time. Suppose he doesn't understand that his emotional problem is from his beliefs. In that case, he won't appreciate his belief that it's okay to get on video chat and why he thinks it's okay to masturbate, i.e. he needs to gain the courage to work with himself to quit video chat.

He could self-monitor during the 24 hours or the next seven days, in the morning, during the day, in the evening or at night, or when he is doing something or when his thoughts are running away.

To the monitor, enter the video chat. Examine those instantly occurring thoughts, leading him to watch the models in the video chat. Paying attention to those little details like where he is, what he is doing, how he feels and what his habits are all lead to looking at something he enjoys, which is the models on that website. If someone is going to stop sitting on video chat and choose to change their life, at first, it may be more accessible or more complex because they are changing a habit, replacing one behaviour with another; there is a transition from one habit to another. Every moment you change something brings a new beginning after the old habit has been dropped. Many reasons against sitting on video chat are already described, and there is no need for many pages and other explanations.

# Strange desires and questions asked by men when sitting on video chat.

I have written below what I have heard from models who work in video chat. Some people sit on video chat, but they don't masturbate; they watch people on a particular video chat site and in between, they do something else.

They may sweat while watching video chat but do other things.

Some people pity the models who work in video chat and pay them for being there.

Some clients love people who work in video chat and love to see their toes and the soles of their feet, i.e. what they haven't seen on that body before.

Some people ask strange questions, such as whether the person has shaved under the arm permanently.

Some people want to understand why it is not good to stay on video chat, so they enter out of curiosity and then join more often until they end up in private.

Customers consider some models to be angels sent by God or they are the "good angels on earth".

# Why can't one understand that it is good to give up to adult video chat models?

Adult video chat is a choice. You don't usually sit on video chat in a bar with friends or on the street. Videochat is restricted; it is used by many people in set-up and enclosed places. Videochat came about because of the internet; without the internet, video chat would not exist. Video chat has become an industry, and millions of people do video chat and work as models in video chat or enter a video chat website model. How does that person look or see themselves when they think they understand what adult video chat is, but they don't keep those promises to stop entering an adult video chat website, promises made to themselves, or maybe to their partner or spouse? Don't be surprised by what I'm writing because there are many situations where married men sit on a video chat website and look at models, even telling their wives that they will stop entering video chat. The problem is that they don't say and talk to other people about such things, or even if they do talk, they only speak to those people who don't criticise them; on the contrary, they even help and encourage each other, rather than finding a solution to stop watching models doing video chat. Let's say that watching.

online video chat in private has a pleasant reason, a sensational reason, a feeling of pleasure or satisfaction, but that leads you to where? Is there a payoff, or do they have an advantage of people looking at models doing video chat? If anyone is wondering why they would try to give up video chat and how to try it, they can find out from the reasons described. The desire to get into video chat comes from curiosity, habit, and the instinct to search, which is started by oneself and by oneself but also arises as a result of the lifestyle one has, one's experiences, and choices.

To quit video chatting, you can try it without someone else's help if you don't want to talk to someone else about the time you spend on video chatting and find solutions to quit video chatting. Or, if he wants a discussion with a specialist in that field who works with people, there are psychologists, psychiatrists or whatever he wants, if he wants to talk to someone. Someone said that if a person changes their lifestyle, for example, their job and work in another country, they can give up that behaviour of going on video chat. Do you believe that? I am unsure because the desire to stay on video chat and go private is in that person's head, heart, and soul. Even if he changed jobs and lives in another country, that desire is in the body; it's in the self; it reappears as an impulse from the feeling that if he took a break, something is missing in that person's life, and after a while, that desire to watch video chat and go private and do what he likes comes back. After a person is satisfied, the urge to keep watching video chat or going private slowly ends, but it's temporary. So that desire will recur; it will come back in that person, as it is with a person addicted to alcohol.

Who needs that drink? After a binge, the next day, he drinks alcohol to recover and to feel better. The video chat would be: Let's go in again and see what girls have come in.

I think some people come in and look at models on a video chat website when they are at work and working on the computer. What I mean is that this is among the first signs of addiction. If you disagree with what I've written here about reducing time spent on video chat and quitting video chat, you don't have to read or understand what I've written. And I have an example. If you want to stop and don't try, you won't be able to stop video chat, even if you want to, or maybe you're thinking, "I'm not quitting now". This may make you feel they are considering quitting, which means they will cease video chatting, but it's not that simple. It's like a beggar begging for years, thinking about quitting, and someone close to him keeps telling him to stop praying. But the beggar hasn't thought about how to try practically or what to do in exchange for the time he goes begging. Or it is the example of an alcoholic. He often wants to give up alcohol and thinks about how to make him give it up, but practically, he doesn't try. It would be simple to do the opposite of what they do when they drink alcohol, i.e. stop buying alcohol. But that's only possible in the movies. The thoughts and beliefs in his head don't allow him to try to give up alcohol because he is full of alcohol in his body and his head. Plants growing in a river with flowing water are bent in the direction of the water flow; downstream, they can't be bent in the opposite direction of the water flow; upstream, that's why the neurons in his head, over time, have also adapted to live with that substance. So, if you're thinking of quitting while consuming alcohol, that

will quit, even if he doesn't feel well from alcohol, because he can't stop swallowing alcohol. It's a habit formed over a long time, and so an alcohol addiction has developed. The same behaviour style is also used by the person on video chat. Still, alcohol addiction versus a form of video chat addiction is treated differently because there are different demands on the body. If someone addicted to video chat will read this book and feels that they want to change and will want to stop being on video chat and find some ways to understand that it is not good to get on video chat, it is possible. At the same time, I'm sure some people will disagree with what was written and how it was written because it goes against their enslaved desires of addiction to seeing something or watching something. How would one begin to give up video chat if one wanted to do that? Or do they expect the change to happen instantly and, in an instant, resolve this frustration by managing to stop attending video chat? But it doesn't work that way; if he doesn't at least have a goal about quitting video chat, I don't see how he can succeed. Many details would need to be adhered to in that goal, even if they initially seem odd. To quit video chatting, if there is no end goal or no plan, they might have to remind themselves, even if they get on a video chat site, that it would be better not to get on that site and quit for good. He could write down some details on a sheet of paper or some of the reasons described above and go back to that page, read them, even when on a video chat site, or write down the questions above and answer them himself.

You need to understand that you need to make a goal. To aim for a goal, you need to set a plan; you could write down the details of how you.

could give up video chatting, and if you do, you may fail, and it may not immediately affect you because the result starts to show after weeks or months. If you set a goal, you will fail to succeed because it takes patience and much motivation.

Something in many people's lives induces the need for sensational things; they want something different from other people, something that makes them feel alive. These people need to do some things like get on video chat or consume alcohol. Still, they don't know that new trials bring new senses, and those senses can make people weak. They can take them captive, and they don't realise that their freedom is lost in the captive mind, so freedom becomes restricted.

The reasons behind the impulses and thoughts of the man who enters the video chat differ from person to person. That is, if you talk to someone who works with the physical presence of people and you talk to three people who are currently chatting or have chatted on video chat, their discussions and thoughts of not speaking on video chat are not identical, nor are their reasons for joining video chat. For example, during this period, someone diagnosed with paranoid schizophrenia, aged 33, went to the practice and, from the first meeting, wanted to find out what her fault was because she had moments when she didn't want to live anymore; she would like to disintegrate. We found out that she was subjected to stringent rules by her parents as a child and that she went through rape and many other unpleasant experiences. And if you're wondering what this example has to do with the book's title, the connection is that I want to show her desire to get better, but her situation is because of her traumas, so it is too late to be an average person. The motivation to do a sure thing is in the thoughts and experiences of life. The reason is to make sure something is in your thoughts.

senses and can explain what happens to people diagnosed with paranoid schizophrenia, such as talking without resolving, i.e. talking to speak, because they are profoundly mentally affected and... and more, I don't want to write. What should be understood from the last lines I noted is that if one thinks that video chat is healthy and that it is okay to sit on video chat, to look at women, to masturbate, to live your life like that, if that is what you want and you are adult and free, then it is your choice. If you don't want to stop watching video chat, then the choice is yours; here, I'm not talking about people who own a video chat business.

People who want to quit video chatting independently and don't try to talk to other people but want to leave would do well to try to make a start in this endeavour. Start small, as you started on video chat, and act in reverse, i.e. stop going in. That would mean that when you get it in your head to enter an adult video chat site or porn site, close the open page and focus on the serious stuff. If you still can't stop joining video chat, ask yourself some questions that will combat the intention to stay on video chat. Below is an example of two questions: Did you do anything to stop video chatting? What did you do to stop video chatting? If you answered these questions, keep the answer in mind. Why remember it? So that you remember it, and it could have a positive effect if you want to stop video chatting

or rephrase that answer, whatever it is.

# Part V- a

How can the author be helpful to people regarding what he

## wrote here about video chat

It can be helpful to write details about models who do video chat to reinforce readers' belief that adult video chat is maladaptive and unhealthy. As is well known, people have different opinions and beliefs towards some things in society and the world, which, to me, the author's approach to helping someone is questioned and always will be because the world is constantly moving and changing. What the author likes does not mean other people like it. From one point of view, what, how and why it was written or for whom it was reported here can be a good thing and have an audience.

The author has tried to bring arguments, in a light-hearted style, to be understood by people who frequent video chat, showing that pursuing video chat is an unhealthy behaviour irrationally and deceptively induced in people who frequently enter video chat, ending up with maladaptive behaviour. For people who are interested in finding out how to do or think about trying to quit video chatting, I wrote.

About video chat addiction, frequency and time spent on video chat, and what a client does on video chat in private. This does not mean that people who frequently log on for a short period to video chat or an adult website, such as porn, are addicted. Clients who enter a video chat site cannot be seen by models on screens in video chat studios or at home; the model considers the user's name and what they write on their page but does not see the person's image. Customers do. However, notice models doing video chat; this means that fantasy or hallucinatory thinking leads them to some satisfaction, psychological and physical. I believe that by offering the visual, their senses can be controlled. In comparison, between a video chat website and a porn site, there is a difference in the presentation and behaviour of the people working on these sites. On a porn site, the action takes place directly and can be viewed as soon as the page is opened, and there are dozens of subject categories to choose from and videos for all types of people, according to their beliefs and thoughts. A porn site can lead to addiction due to the desire for satisfaction one wants to feel. An adult site is also accessed by many teenagers, who form the belief that it is pleasurable to be on an adult site where they can be satisfied. Emotions are behind these behaviours of seeking satisfaction and pleasure, which bring out an affective reaction that changes the person's body, beliefs, and rational and subconscious thinking. These can show a healthy or unhealthy emotion, reflecting the person's beliefs about whether or not to believe that thing. Addiction is a disease that sometimes cannot be understood. I say this because, as I have written before, there are people who are addicted, for example.

a substance, alcohol, video chat models, or adult websites, and at the root of these behaviours are beliefs influenced by the person's emotions, senses, and feelings, which are observable and can be seen from the outside. This would mean that there are different reasons why a person enters a video chat site, and each person has another reason for seeking relaxation and satisfaction.

For example, if someone has had a hard day at work, they may think that after working hours, it is good to go to a video chat model website to relax, knowing that there are people there who are pleasing to the eye of customers. Another example might be that, after a stressful day at work after hours, she wants to spend her evenings in bars drinking alcohol. The author seeks to show healthy and unhealthy thinking, i.e., rational and irrational. Even if there are mistakes perhaps in the wording, the intention is to help people who intuitively feel that it is good to stop video chatting; I have already written for people who are addicted to video chat and want to stop video chatting, and these people do not know what to do to stop video chatting. It would be good to talk to someone regularly so that they are aware of when they enter and why they enter various video chat sites.

## Why do some people frequently enter or are addicted to video chat?

People want to see some things, not knowing they are harmful, being led by the senses. Video chat is an industry with millions of customers and users, and if it weren't for the customers who frequently enter these video chat websites, there wouldn't be people working as models in video chat. Some models have said they have loyal customers who come in frequently at certain times of the 24 hours, and the models are there for them. Who are these people who often enter a video chat site? Those who have various reasons to join and some of the many who have access to the internet.

# Can video chat attract civilised and disciplined people?

Video chatting can lead the human psyche to mental disorders with unhealthy and go severe, and harmful emotional consequences. At the beginning of this topic, I think for sure about civilised and disciplined People, be those who spend much time on video chat and due to the time on video chat and the desires they have after a while, they pass to another level of thinking. They are led with their mind to do bad things too, but not only civilised and disciplined People enter on video chat. In my description, I will write about two parts in people's thinking: a good part and a bad part; here, I am writing about an element of the wrong part. It is about people who look on video chat not only at girls over the age of 18 but at girls under the age of 18. people who look for girls under the age of 18 are also doing bad things, looking for underage young girls for sexual relations, kidnapping young girls and so on. These people you don't recognise or notice if you pass on the street and you look at these people to be interested in girls under the age of 18, and even if you are talking to a paedophile and discussing a particular topic, you can't tell that this person is a paedophile, or is trafficking for prostitution because he has that intelligence to have that discussion without being suspected of being a paedophile, There are girls kidnapped for

Paedophiles, these people pay big money to have sex with underage girls so as not to be noticed, are people who can afford to pay other people to approach or kidnap young girls under the age of 18 to be sold on.

I write this way because people watch a lot of video chat and, after a while, look for young girls in other places, for example, on the street or at school. People who look at girls under 18 on the internet and have desires how to approach them are people who manage to attract the attention of some kinds of underage girls and seduce them; these people are the kind of people who do not recognise this fact, to look for young girls under the age of 18, to kidnap them, or to have sex unless there is clear evidence. Otherwise, they will never recognise it. These people are careful and aware not to talk about young girls so they won't be suspected and show that hidden side. What I am writing about is that I am not referring to all people who watch video chat who want to meet young girls under 18.

Do you think it's civilised and disciplined for people to do bad things or watch video chat? I'm convinced, but that doesn't mean YOU are convinced like me, and I don't mean all civilised or disciplined people do bad things.

I believe that the Devil also selects People favoured by God. There are more words in this statement or explanation that are not worth writing because it's better to stick to your opinion. After all, you don't think of the same example of People being favoured by something I'm thinking of.

What about Civilized and Disciplined People who often enter video chat sites?

They want to watch the girls on those sites. They choose to watch video chatting models shake their asses to attract customers to earn money. As I write here, I am thinking of writing a few things. For example, it is impossible to understand some unhealthy behaviours. I am interested in how to get sick Imagination, Stupidity, Fantasy, Hallucination and delusion out of the heads of people who often enter video chat. Maybe someone is wondering, for example, what Illusion I am writing about here or what Hallucination. What do I mean by these words? People who spend much time on video chat could say they want to look at girls, and that's all to enter on video chat. "You die because you only desire to enter the video chat." You don't see that your desire is hallucinating. This desire for video chat leads the man to a satisfaction that creates addiction and neurological and mental problems, and after a while, it requires medical treatment. But that it will end up in medication is not understood before.

A civilised Man has his civilised habits and sees other people as uncivilised, but he does not see himself as rough and does terrible things. Does anyone believe that civilised and disciplined people who do bad things think they are overlooked or feel like they are doing bad things? Bad things for them sometimes become a habit, or it has nothing if they have done something wrong to someone. Suppose anyone is reading and has come this far. In that case, they will wonder what bad things I am referring to: how are people who show themselves to be civilised and notice other people who are uncivilised and make remarks to those people that they are crude and want to be civilised when they consider people who show themselves civilised. But why do civilised people do bad things? Smokers who leave hundreds of cigarette butts wherever they want, consumers of others.

Prohibited substances and alcohol, people who destroy other people's things, Cars, Houses, land near the house, and valuable objects, which have value for other people, have reasons to do these things because they don't care. They don't care, or they destroy other people's things or other worse deeds. Someone will say that the examples I wrote are unsuitable for civilised people; I mean those people who speak very nicely and are disciplined but do not care about other people's things and destroy them intentionally or out of revenge. A civilised person can say, how dare he speak to me in such a tone? I will show him or them to suffer. Such a Man will find ways to harm other people intentionally.

# Are adult video chat and porn sites healthy or beneficial?

My opinion is that these adult sites are unhealthy and are a great harm to many people around the world.

But these sites are no longer only accessed by adults, I think, and are accessed by many young people under 18. These young people have access to and conditions for a video chat site, and I don't encourage those under 18 to enter a video chat site. The people who benefit from video chat are the models who do it; they are visitors who have managed to satisfy themselves and look at someone on a monitor. It is not enough to talk or say that it is not good to enter a video chat site or porn site. It is necessary to understand what kind of thoughts has in the head to join video chat and convince oneself that it is worth entering a video chat site or a porn site and why one gets addicted to video chat or a porn website,= lack of satisfaction.

I have observed that People who have mental problems or different illnesses or who develop early in life a mental or chronic issue, such as addiction, which they do not treat and worsen during life or severe Depression. Generally, these people understand only after treatment has begun.

Medication, after which they talk to other people about their health problems and after a while, they become frustrated with the drug treatment transcribed as treatment. So if you get there on medication and have some issues, a person may wonder, what does video chat have to do with the mental problem or a porn site? Some people work for years in adult video chat studios or porn sites. Yes, but for these people, it is a job that has become normal and similar to an employee's routine. But as a customer on one or more video chat sites, after a few hours of work, thinks it is good to get into video chat among the things he has to do, video chat is a misunderstood evil. The problem I see for video chat customers, related to their beliefs of thinking it is good to get on video chat, wasting their time on these damn and bad needy sites that don't force anyone to get on or use them, would be a hallucinatory, imaginary, momentary mind and contained by deprivation in the lives of video chat customers after a while it becomes a routine a habit. So then, what is it in Man that so many people enter a video chat site? = **It is evil in Man that has good parts and bad parts; it is love that has good parts and harmful elements.** Could it be a connection between Man and Cognitive Imagination that leads to video chat? Video chatting for visitors is a trick, a waste of time, and a disappointment or a hoax.

Affective feelings are some of those reasons that lead a person to frequently enter a video chat site or porn site or be in a blind, misguided desire. And what I mean when I write affective senses: I'll start with the word Sense: to feel something for someone or something, from here at the beginning, intervenes throughout life, curiosity.

And they are trying new things that move what a person feels in their body when they look at a picture or video chat.

People who often enter video chat because of their thoughts and beliefs and because of their uncontrolled and misunderstood senses are misled by themselves to enter video chat sites that millions of people visit. It is true that a video chat or porn site does not ask anyone to join that site and does not force anyone to enter; this means that people's minds and senses have become manipulated by themselves. For people who enter a porn site, it is pleasurable; it is a pleasure, it is satisfaction; I believe it is a fantasy, an illusion, and a hallucination for many people who waste their time on these sites. Where are the people who work in porn? Where are the millions of people who work on porn sites? If anyone has arrived and read these lines, maybe for 1 hour, agree with what I have written below, and I will pass down some written words I agree with about porn.

- Porn is unhealthy and completely worth ignoring.

- Porn is a nervous evil.

- Porn is something that changes People's senses and lives into deceptive and misleading sensations, perceptions and feelings.

- Porn means hedonism

- Porn is not love.

- It's good to hate the thought and intention before you go in to look at a porn site.

It is good to discuss with someone about watching video chat in detail because video chatting is unhealthy and leads to a form of addiction. Still, this addiction is not about watching, which leads to more maladaptive body behaviours.

If you are a man, you may have noticed women discussing many things and relationships with men in detail with other women. For example, why do I say so because out of 10 clients at the practice, six are female, and indeed, they discuss in detail and find solutions to problems that are? Therefore, if a person who often enters video chat understands that the reason for wanting to join for a long time is to feel good if he wants to quit video chat, then that person will not understand that his feelings and desire to masturbate lead him to enter video chat, in short, he enters video chat because, in the head of that person, there are more personal reasons of his satisfaction.

# The Role of Imagination and Video Chat

Does imagination have anything to do with people who video chat often?

The definition of imagination is complex and of many kinds; I will write about how I think about imagination on video chat as I believe it has to do with the human mind. Imagination can change the beliefs of many people into completely unhealthy thinking and desires about video chatting, as well as many men's opinions about women. The desire to be on video chat can start from curiosity, a thought, an idea, or an image somewhere with someone on the internet about video chat that is a click away. This imagination with cognitive affectivity is also related to memory about events experienced in the present and optional selection of things. Imagination is an intellectual process of knowing realities, the future and the possible; imagination can move with the mind in many realms, far from reality sometimes. Imagination contributes to the extent of future and fulfilment satisfaction in people who enter video chat. A person on video chat can create an image in his mind to be convinced that it is worth looking at the models doing video chat in certain positions, for example, why different positions because that's why there are their models doing video chat to move for their customers and customers observing these positions, feel a pleasure.

And a desire for satisfaction through masturbation, for example. People need imagination; often, imagination in the human mind has a trajectory or path, which can be healthy or unhealthy for many people. It would be suitable for people to be more careful about who they think about or expect to be on video chat.

# Is it worth paying a monthly fee on an online platform to look at pictures of adults?

The image of that picture is to attract as many people as possible. That picture looks seductive and pleasing. It is one of the dozens of images made to show what some people want to look for, from a painting that can start the way to a desire for pleasure and having the need to feel intense sensations. Those intense sensations can lead the person to a state of joy or incline the person to be attracted to and feel pleasure. I can't oppose someone's desires and imagination if they want to pay for an internet subscription to access pictures of adults. Whoever pays is not just looking at images of adults. Perhaps they are looking at something else, so I can only write what I think about people who spend a monthly fee on a website to look at some intimate pictures. The desire and persuasion of people to pay a monthly subscription on an online website via the internet and look at adults, in my view, looks mind-boggling; the mind of those people if they prefer to pay a monthly amount of money and also look at adults who put their pictures, and videos on the internet, are pleasures and sensations of the country, they fell more different, and they like how they think, it means that something is wrong. However, this could be more understandable.

Pleasures are a step of unbridled desire and not understanding the unbridled attraction from the pictures and videos they watch. Paying a monthly fee on a website seems to be another form of video chat because there are adult videos, too. People who spend a monthly payment on an internet platform understand what they want because they virtually choose that person through the internet and choose to stay to look at that person. Let's say they prefer to pay a monthly fee to look at a person they adore or like in the pictures they look at, and that person is satisfied or content to look at those pictures of one person; it seems like they are in a virtual relationship, or has fallen in love with that person through what they see in the images. Probably over time, people who pay a fee to have access to intimate photos will surely convince themselves that it's a mistake. Stop paying those fees on some adult sites to look at human flesh. Be patient that you'll get to feel it when you feel it on your skin physically; then no, you'll still need to look at those pictures if you get to touch a loved one physically. I wonder if this is sane in that person who pays a monthly fee to look at photos of other adults?

# Some details about the author

The person who wrote this book wishes to remain anonymous. Information about the person who wrote here is optional. What is more important is how it was written and the effect on people who want to know how to quit video chatting.

There would be many reasons to write about this author's decision this way, and below I write one of the reasons.

The author may be wanted, threatened or hurt for the way words are used. These words can be interpreted as detrimental to those with a video chat business, even though the author of this book is not attacking or accusing people who work in these places or have video chat enterprises. Given that people have different opinions and beliefs, there will always be discussion, criticism, and disagreement about how it was written in this book. Still, there may be good opinions as well. The reality about people who spend much time with models doing video chat is harsh and visible but hidden from many people for many reasons.

I'm writing to help people who overdo their time on video chat and who intuitively feel they want to stop spending time there, and I hope I can do that to understand these feelings that are part of that person's life or that person's life. I wonder how many people.

With time, some will manage to give up video chat, out of all the diversity of those minds' ways of thinking and socialising, and there will be people who will try to propose giving it up. I'm not claiming that this book is the solution to the lifelong relapses that a man who spends money on video chat has and wants to stop but can't. It may be one of the solutions. And I don't care what you think about me; I don't care what you say and why you say it because you don't know me; it's none of my business what people who don't know me think about me, but I can say in short that those who do know me, and they are people from different countries, people I have worked and collaborated with, who respect me and not for what I am, but for the things I have done and how I have done them. And I'm still remembered; I know that because I keep in touch with these people I've worked with.

I have written these lines and reasons as I knew from myself, from my mind. What is written here is not copied from other sources, but I researched and read from various sources. I read books, formed ideas, and noted further; I read articles online, watched videos, and listened to what people in business or engaged in the video chat industry said. But, most importantly, I wrote for people who want to quit video chat and need help figuring out how to do it. It's like how some people who are addicted to alcohol want to leave but don't know how to start. And I'm sure it's hard to give up an addiction. I haven't given the book to other people who are famous for their opinion of what I've written here; that doesn't mean I'm a secretive man; it means I'm meticulous; I'm a man who physically works every day and doesn't spend much time online. In overall, I spent more time in front of my laptop while writing this from start to finish. I am not a specialist in the grammar of the language of my country because I have spent almost two decades living in another country with a different culture and am not a literary man. I am a man who believes in freedom, in which great care is needed in what, how and when you speak about something, and I have learned that silence and patience solve many things in human life. That is why freedom is uncertain and misunderstood. I prefer the freedom to choose what to do and how to do things where I have a purpose or goal. Sometimes, the ups and downs of life kill a man's meaning or dream, thwarting the attainment of that desired goal or objective. Some problems and misunderstandings come to be perceived by men as obstacles. The burdens of life that man fails to control, such as some habits or a form of addiction, destroy man's happiness slowly and surely. I haven't had habits of sitting on video chat or hiding. I have not spent much time on sites with women, and I want to show others that I know the solution to not sitting in a video chat.

# Below are some questions with solutions which can be requested from this book

## A few questions are similar to the description throughout the book, but it's good to have them here for clarity.

### To whom is this book written?

It's for people who want to understand that looking at an adult and video chat site can lead to addiction, and the word addiction can be subtly understood in many forms; I'm talking about that addiction that creates health problems, those problems that are shallow profile and not taken seriously and treated until too late.

## What do I want to show?

About the time spent with models on video chat and the money spent privately online because someone on their monitor is looking at someone else far away in a particular place prepared and arranged. Those models are there because they know someone will pay that money privately, and anyone who spends money on models doing video chat behaves unhealthily.

## Why would anyone read this book?

To find out the reasons described and because some reasons might be helpful. There are many reasons for someone to want to read, such as out of curiosity, pleasure, self-interest, or perhaps for self-analysis or study.

# Why is this book needed?

To understand that it is not healthy what you feel and think before entering a video chat site, or to discuss long periods with models on an adult site or video chat website with people who work there. This little book is a must, but not for everyone.

# Can this book matter? Can it be necessary?

It's up to anyone who wants to know what it says, and I'm not saying there are incredible and unheard-of words here, no, not at all. The book may help people who want to understand what I have written.

*The following text below* is copied from an article published in 2017 about one person's experience as a video chat model. The text shows the reality of the connection between clients and video chat models. The model who is speaking did video chat during her student days. I removed terms described as intimate parts. They are descriptions of the model who did video chat at that time. I have only included the model's history.

# Below is the description of the person who worked as a model in video chat.

I think learning about sex is about education. For me, this experience helped me self-discover what I like and what I don't. But that's not all. Clients want to see that the girl likes it. Even though they know she's faking it, they want to see her moaning, enjoying more. It's like a theatre show, only it's a little more...Porn. They know very well that I mimic orgasms, and sometimes, they ask me to do the same thing over and over again.

And I only do it if I see the token amount in my account. I do it for the money and have no embarrassment; there is no danger.

From that point of view, it's better than being a porn actress, where you can get STDS. Why do men like to see that the girl likes it? Because it seems to them that they've given her pleasure.

But although they pay, she is in control. Someone said that everything in this world is about sex except sex; sex is about control. That's precisely what I see in video chat. In video chat, the models are the ones who have the power. If they want to, they do video chat; if they don't, they don't.

He thinks he controls me by giving me money, but I hold his fantasy. I will do what he asks and give him the satisfaction of mimicking a resounding orgasm that looks like it came from him, that he caused me that pleasure. Or, I'll keep him in check and discreetly suggest that a more resounding orgasm means more money. Video chat is a power play, and the model may or may not be able to retain a client.

If she's talented, there will be men looking only for her. And it's not about the porn stuff she does but some chemistry between the model and her client, like in life. It's an emotional connection that happens a lot between the model and the client. Not to mention people who fall in love with girls and want to take them as wives. They still decide if they will get to know each other, but I don't think some models want to know the men sitting on the video chat.

They will entertain this fantasy if they want to succeed, but they will never put it into practice. Playing on customers' emotions is their form of power, the girls'. Others have asked me for sadomasochistic stuff that I've refused. This is one of the advantages of video chat versus porn or classic prostitution; you can say no.

Some girls don't want to take their clothes off and prefer to talk to their customers; some have been loyal to them for years. Some are simply men who don't listen to their wives at home, unloved men who want to chat, too.

But many want to stick with fantasy. What, you haven't seen people who say they want a relationship but don't? That they have a relationship fantasy? The ones who call you and keep you in check but sometimes don't even motivate themselves to come to have sex on Saturday night? I've seen it happen, too; I've been in that kind of relationship myself.

So that's it. Some people just want fantasy, even the craziest one, and that's what we video chat girls are for.

Through this example, the author shows the relationship between the model doing the video chat and the men who come in and talk to them. Clients want to avoid admitting they spend their money on fantasy and nonsense because you can't have those models doing video chat. I read somewhere that men, as they get older and older, want to have as many offspring as possible, even if they have children, and they don't wish to take care of those children. Video chat clients who tried physically surprising a model after spending much time on video chat were left with regrets. There have been video chat models who have had clients for months at a time, and after a while, those men have said they were in their city doing video chat and were disappointed because they didn't meet those models doing video chat. There's money in it; it's the money the models do video chat for. Some men went to look for models in the city where they said they do video chat and got a response like the one in the following picture.

That would translate: I didn't call you to come on video chat, honey, and I didn't ask you to visit me in the town where I live.

# Conclusion

I think it's hard to take what's written here thoughtfully, but it's easier for many people not to believe what's written because it can destabilise their own beliefs. If someone has spent time on video chat, it is not a disaster in their life, but it would be good to understand that it is pointless and people can do anything else in their lifetime. The body always speaks to us like an inner voice; it is an age-specific voice that feels something specific and looks like an incomprehensible feeling in each person, according to his character and personality. If people take the time to discuss this behaviour or understand that it is not good to sit on a video chat site, they will go further towards giving up that behaviour; that's why I think in this book, some words can be seen in many forms - unconvincing, wrong form - or maybe in a favourable sense by people who are against adult video chat. I've written about what happens when one enters a video chat site and when someone is on video chat. People who get on video chat, because of the misunderstood and uncontrolled impulse reached in the body as well as the desire that sometimes comes instantly, quickly come to have the belief that it is okay to get on video chat and to believe that it is unhealthy is even more unlikely. To avoid frequenting an adult video chat site, it would be better for those people to be in a sexual relationship with someone and being in a relationship or marriage can dissolve tension and frustration more easily than looking at a naked person as a model in a monitor. We forget the situation we have created, and sometimes the reason is hidden within us, and we don't realise or blame someone else for the hardships we have had in our lives. No one has power over you if you are a free person. Humans are solitary thinkers in our minds; we make the decisions and choose to do those things. I believe that if we gain peace, harmony and balance in our mind, it can lead to living that way in life as well. I understand that beautiful things and beautiful people have their price, sooner or later, and that price sometimes is high, paying with suffering and time, that time that is too short.

The book reveals the reality of the people who frequent video chat sites and those who work as models in video chat studios or at home because I listened to interviews with many such people, from which I formed an opinion. I've heard models talk about their clients, saying that some are freaks. I've added the word "weird" to why people who frequently join video chat sites traditionally give up and talk to others to convince themselves that staying on a video chat site is incorrect. I have written several times that it would be better to keep on video chat. Some of the reasons described can affect some people if those reasons are understood. It may help if one re-reads that reason again, which is exciting and may change something even if it sometimes seems absurd.

Finally, I thank you, reader, wherever you are, for your time, patience, and curiosity about this little book! There may be many mistakes, and I admit I am not perfect, but I learn from the people I talk to and know how to be heard and understood. It is not easy to work with a person's psyche, nor are people the same; each person is unique and deserves the respect they deserve.

Freedom is not free. Someone always has to pay the ultimate price, and man threatens some people's freedom.

It is possible without video chat; it is not a necessity to

enter such a website; there is no need for that!

If the way I have written has upset anyone, I apologise. I write my opinions here; that's all I knew to write in this little book.

In the end, I'll write a little advice for people who read and enter a video chat site, and not all people who read this little book enter or frequent video chat sites.

My advice is: **Don't visit** a video chat site to look at the models. These models are only there to earn money. They are entirely different from what you imagine they might be in reality, and I can give you an example. The models who do video chat in real life look different from what they look on a video chat website. I saw with my own eyes when I was in another country the same person who was a video chat model. I saw her on the street in the country where she was working as a video chat model. She looked completely different in the appearance of her face and hair. Don't go on those sites.

Who does video chat, and that's it? Please stop. **Ignore** these people who work as video chat models or on adult websites. These people can be whatever they want to be, but it's okay to **ignore them.**

I understand the Meaning of Fantasy, Illusion, and Hallucination as a significant factor in the minds of people who frequently enter video chat.

# A few requirements from the Author if there is anyone who wants

## to contact him

If there will be anyone who may wish to contact me about what was written in this book, I need the address of the person at work if they are an employee of a state organisation. I will ask for the necessary data to convince me they are serious, namely a legal online website if they have one, a phone number, email address and the contact person's name. If these requirements are not met, I will not respond further. At the end of this book, I will leave an active email address where your questions can be answered, should there be any questions.

Email: cristib045@gmail.com

# Bibliography

*Guide to Rational Emotive and Behavioural Therapy*, Table 1. page 11

Internet - YouTube, Models who talked about their video chat experience on *In the Mirror*

Book *The Illusion of Money*, Kyle Cease
The book *You Can Heal Your Life* by Louise Hay. I took from her inspirational ideas and wrote in my own words. Psychologies magazine, In an article published in 2017, writes about a model who recounts her experiences while working as a video chat model.
*Wikipedia* - Free encyclopedia, **illusion**

# About the Author

The author of this book works as a Psychologist Specialising in Clinical Psychology and Cognitive Behavioral Psychotherapy and works on his private cabinet; over time, he has come to observe and talk with people in general; men have a hard time admitting and are ashamed to talk about spending a lot of time on the internet looking at video chat models. This behaviour of looking after women over the internet for an extended period of years, more than ten years, can create a profoundly unhealthy form of addiction to looking on various video chat sites at different video chat models. The models who do video chat are from different cultures and are located on multiple video chat sites worldwide. Behind this behaviour, men have miscellaneous reasons and senses why they are spending time and money for models who do video chat; however, the author of the book finds out that most of the men who are spending time watching models on video chat cannot stop even if they want and said I would not watch models and spend money anymore, after a while they come back. The author of this book works as a Psychologist Specialising in Clinical Psychology and Cognitive Behavioral Psychotherapy and works on his private cabinet; over time, he has come to observe and talk with people in general; men have a hard time admitting and are ashamed to talk about spending a lot of time on the internet looking at video chat models. This behaviour of looking after women over the internet for an extended period of years, more than ten years, can create a profoundly unhealthy form of addiction to looking on various video chat sites at different video chat models. The models who do video chat are from different cultures and are located on multiple video chat sites worldwide. Behind this behaviour, men have miscellaneous reasons and senses why they are spending time and money for models who do video chat; however, the author of the book finds out that most of the men who are spending time watching models on video chat cannot stop even if they want and said I would not watch models and spend money anymore, after a while they come back.